# AN UNSHAKABLE MIND

IRH Press

**BOOKS**
IRH PRESS
New York

ISBN: 978-1-942125-91-4

Printed in Canada

Second Edition

# AN UNSHAKABLE MIND

## MIND

*How to Overcome
Life's Difficulties*

EL CANTARE

# RYUHO OKAWA

IRH PRESS

# Contents

## CHAPTER FOUR
# Various Types of Evil Spirits

## CHAPTER FIVE
# Confronting Evil Spirits

## CHAPTER SIX

# An Unshakable Mind

# Preface

This book, *An Unshakable Mind*, teaches a method to build a great character that is founded upon a spiritual worldview.

An unshakable mind cannot be acquired overnight. You first need to construct a solid base, like the part of an iceberg that remains hidden underwater. For this reason, I have devoted the whole second chapter of this book to explaining what I call "The Principle of Accumulation."

In Chapter Three, "Confronting Distress in Life," I talked about the manifestations of an unshakable mind. In Chapter Four, "Various Types of Evil Spirits," and Chapter Five, "Confronting Evil Spirits," I have analyzed the causes of suffering and written concrete ways of overcoming them.

I hope and pray that this book will provide light in the darkness to guide those who are seeking and living in accordance with Buddha's Truth.

*Ryuho Okawa*
*Master & CEO of Happy Science Group*
*June 1997*

# CHAPTER ONE

# The Iceberg of Life

# 1

## The Foundations for Life

In this book, I would like to discuss how to overcome life's difficulties and sufferings from a variety of angles. The central theme is "an unshakable mind."

I would like to begin by considering the foundations for life. Whether or not firm foundations have been established is of vital importance to everything. This is as true for an individual as it is for a large corporation; without a firm base, an individual or company will be weak. The same can be said about any type of work. In every aspect of life, strong foundations are important.

For example, I think that the main purpose of school education is to lay strong foundations for your life. Those who have negative views of education systems often criticize education in schools as a waste of time, saying that individuals should be free to study whatever they like and however much they want. However, it cannot be denied that a well-rounded education is beneficial in creating firm foundations for life.

During the course of our lives, we have to make decisions and take action on many different issues. In order to do that, we need information, motivation, and basic skills on which we base our decisions and actions. People cannot make decisions or take action without having accumulated these things. Cooking is a good example of this. Housewives can cook every day because they have the basic skills of cooking. They have a basic idea of cooking and know dozens or even hundreds of recipes. That is why they can make meals every day smoothly.

Another example is driving. To be able to drive, you need to know the traffic rules and regulations and how to cope with various situations such as driving on slopes, in the rain, at night, and passing oncoming cars in narrow streets. This knowledge provides you with the necessary information to make decisions. If you are ignorant of the rules, you will not know what to do when you meet an oncoming car or how to make a right or left turn. Only when you know the traffic rules and regulations can you drive correctly.

In the same way, it is very important to have firm foundations in life. The more solid and dense your foundations are, the more profound your decisions and actions will be. You should sometimes look at yourself and ask if you are making daily efforts to build the foundations on which you base your life. If your foundations are inadequate, you will find that things do not go smoothly in many situations.

Foundation building should not just be limited to childhood. Even as an adult, you should continue to build your foundations tirelessly. A tree grows bigger and bigger because it never ceases to absorb water and nourishment through its roots. It continues to absorb them even after it has grown tall; otherwise, it would die within a week. Trees that live for hundreds of years ceaselessly absorb these essentials through their roots.

This applies to human beings, too. You cannot say that since you are already a "full-grown tree," you do not need water or nourishment; actually, it is important that you continue to take in what you need on a daily basis in order to build your foundations. Human beings have a tendency to place importance on producing, but if they focus only on producing without absorbing, before long, they will become exhausted.

The same can be said for professions. For instance, there is a world of difference between pharmacists who continue to acquire and absorb new information about medicine and those who have not acquired new knowledge since graduating from university. This is also true of company employees. There is a world of difference between those who simply do the work they are given and those who constantly study, acquiring new information about the economy or other knowledge that helps them do a better job.

This difference is especially apparent among engineers. Those who are always experimenting day after day, looking to improve their skills, will eventually succeed in developing new forms of technology. Doctors are another example. A doctor who studies various things to understand people's sufferings will earn a good reputation.

So rather than being satisfied with establishing your foundations once and then neglecting them, it is all the more important that you strive daily to build the foundations of your life. Even if you don't get immediate results, building foundations that will give you good results in three, five, or even ten years is more important than anything.

# 2

# The Shape of an Iceberg

The foundations of your life can be compared to an iceberg that drifts across the ocean. The part of the iceberg that is above the water only accounts for 10 or 20 percent of the whole iceberg; underwater is the rest of the iceberg, which is a massive block of ice. The iceberg may seem small if you just look at the part that is visible, but the part that is underwater is surprisingly large.

An iceberg needs a large base to be stable enough to float on water. I believe you should learn from this and try to be like an iceberg yourself. The thing you can learn from an iceberg is its stability. Instead of the entire iceberg being exposed above the surface of the ocean, a large section of it always remains underwater. The water displaced by the submerged part of the iceberg applies an upward buoyancy force on the iceberg to keep it afloat.

Similarly, in life, the bigger the part beneath the surface, the greater its buoyancy force. The part that is underwater corresponds to the part of you that is not seen by others. Everyone has an "outer side" that others can see and an "inner side" that others cannot see. Usually, people with a much larger ratio of the "inner side" are considered people of great character. You do not call someone a great figure if you can easily see through them. A truly great person gives off a reserved but impressive light; they possess something profound within them.

In the end, how great of a person you are depends on the part of you that remains hidden from others, namely, your foundations. Those who reveal only a fraction of themselves but keep a vast amount hidden underneath have stability. So, when building the foundations of your life, remember to model after the shape of an iceberg.

# 3

## Withstanding Life's Storms

One of the characteristics of an iceberg is its stability in the face of storms. Even though an iceberg floats on the sea, it remains as stable as terra firma. It resembles an aircraft carrier in that you can walk on it without feeling any movement. This is the secret to withstanding the storms of life. Those who have accumulated a solid foundation in their lives will be able to withstand any criticism or censure and endure suffering or setbacks.

It is often said that you should delve into novels during adolescence. This is because by reading novels, you can learn about someone else's life and experience it as your own. You cannot change the environment in which you were born and raised, and there is a limit to the number of people you can meet in the course of your life. In most cases, people experience joy, sadness, and pain within their own small circle. Through novels, however, you can learn about the lives of people living in totally different environments. By identifying with the main character, you are able to learn more deeply about life.

In this way, novels can enrich your store of wisdom about life. As you read the characters facing and overcoming various difficulties, you can identify with them and become determined to face your own problems in just the same way because most sufferings in life have been novelized. The most common problems people face and suffer from are things like school entrance exams, employment, marriage, and illness. Many of these problems have been made the subject of novels by talented writers.

If you decide to read and learn from these books, you will be able to solve your problems with the help of people with a higher perspective. The causes of your distress and difficulties will appear quite obvious to a person with a more profound understanding of human life. Sometimes, just a single book can provide you with enough clues to help you solve your own problems so you won't have to continue to suffer needlessly.

You can learn not only from novels but also from history books, too. Of course, no one has ever lived an identical life to yours, but many people have stood in a similar position to yours. Knowing how these people managed to overcome their difficulties will teach you methods for solving the problems in your life.

You can learn various things from historical figures. For example, from Nobunaga Oda*, you can learn his passion; his accomplishments, decision-making, and dynamic energy were as if he were cutting the Gordian knot. In the case of

---

*Nobunaga Oda, Hideyoshi Toyotomi, and Ieyasu Tokugawa were Japanese warlords in 16th to 17th century Japan.

Hideyoshi Toyotomi, you can learn from his overflowing wit, quick thinking, and ingenious accomplishments. From Ieyasu Tokugawa, you can learn wisdom. The feudal system he built lasted for almost 300 years. It lasted that long because it was backed by his great wisdom regarding people and social structures. By studying Ieyasu's management skills, you can learn ways to keep a company running.

Besides novels and history books, there is another kind of writing that comforts people in times of suffering and sadness. That is the works of great poets. When you encounter a poem that moves you, your heart may find peace as you find someone else describing your situation and expressing the same feelings. Great poets have a very clear view of life. They see through people's lives. Their poems bring peace and relaxation to the reader's heart.

The same is true of art. A beautiful painting or drawing can bring much comfort to people's hearts. As you sip a cup of coffee in a café, a beautiful painting on the wall will enrich your mind. Art can sometimes heal the wounds people carry in their hearts. The same applies to great musical pieces. When you listen to a masterpiece, the vibrations of your soul become attuned to the refined vibrations of the composer, and the music transports you to a world of great peace.

You can also solve your problems from a religious standpoint. If you cannot find solutions in novels, history books, or art, you may find guideposts for life in the words of great saints or religious leaders of the past. You can find where you are going wrong through their words. Shakyamuni Buddha, Jesus Christ, and Confucius were all great teachers of life. That is because they were outstanding in their ability to see through people's problems and provide prescriptions for solving them. So, when your worries are going round and round inside your head, you can dissolve them by reading and studying the philosophies of these great teachers.

This is one of the objectives of this book. I am writing this book in the hopes that people whose minds are constantly agitated, who are in the midst of worries, or who are always experiencing ups and downs can find salvation. If even a single sentence of this book brings peace and support to the readers, I will be satisfied.

To sum up what I have been saying here, learning from the wisdom of great figures and artists will enlarge the foundations of your life that lie beneath the surface, which in turn will help you withstand the storms of life. So, try to accumulate more wisdom so that you can withstand them. Remember to have strong foundations that will not be affected by the wind, no matter how fiercely it blows across the surface of the ocean.

# 4

## A Sense of Great Stability

From the natural wonder of an iceberg, we need to learn a sense of great stability. Most of the sorrows and sufferings experienced in life originate from a lack of stability. Out of the people you have met so far, whom did you most admire? What kind of people did you respect and consider great? Did you ever think that someone whose mind was unsteady and whose moods swung constantly from anger to sadness to happiness all in a single day was admirable? You probably did not want to be like them.

People you look up to as your ideal are the kind of people you want to be like. These people have a common trait— there is a sense of stability in the way they live. This is one of the secrets of becoming a leader. The quality required of a leader is a sense of stability. It is not the stability of a train that simply runs along the rails but a stability that stands strong amid problems, no matter what kinds of trouble they are confronted with.

As I have already explained, one of the factors that create this sense of stability is the accumulation of wisdom. Those who possess this stability have a store of wisdom; they know what kind of problems people in the past faced, the circumstances behind those problems, and how they solved them. They can then apply the same methods to solve their own difficulties.

At such times, it is important to be able to see from a higher perspective. If your emotions are unstable, changing from day to day, it is because you are wrestling with a problem and you are in a deadlock; you cannot tell who is winning, you or the problem. Until the game is over, you have no idea if you are the winner or the loser. As a result, your mind wavers.

Take sumo wrestling as an example. Do you think you can win against a sumo wrestling's grand champion? In almost every case, an ordinary person would have absolutely no chance against a professional sumo wrestler; he would be pushed out of the ring and lose the match in an instant. The gap in skills is simply too great. Professional sumo wrestlers practice in the ring every day, so they develop powerful muscles, do weight gain, and improve their speed to become strong. When faced with someone like this, an ordinary person will not even think of defeating them. Naturally, you will become powerless and be defeated even more quickly than expected.

The same can be said of encountering troubles in life. If you do not have much confidence in yourself, the people you are having problems with may seem much stronger and extremely evil. It will seem like your problems are very serious. As a result, you will go weak at the knees, as if you are facing a great sumo wrestler.

However, if you become a great champion yourself, you can solve your problems with surprising ease. You must know this. So, before you start worrying about how to solve your problems, develop the strength of a grand champion so that any problems will seem like minor matters that can easily be solved. Then you can easily deal with them, like dealing with a small load. A load that is too heavy for an ordinary person to carry on his back and take ten steps can be carried by a single hand of a professional sumo wrestler.

If people train themselves, they will develop in stature. When it comes to physical training, there is a limit to how much you can increase your abilities. For example, in a hundred-meter sprint, a fast runner may finish in a little under 10 seconds, but even a slow runner can finish in under 20 seconds. So, in terms of physical strength, the difference in the abilities is twofold at most.

However, when it comes to inner strength, there is a huge difference between an exceptional person and an ordinary person. For example, there is a huge difference between the intelligence of Socrates and that of an ordinary person, just as there is a huge difference between the wisdom of Shakyamuni Buddha and that of an ordinary priest.

The more you train your inner self, the greater your ability and brilliance. There are no limits on how much these can increase. There are limits to how much you can develop your physical strength, but your inner strength can be developed a thousand-fold or even ten thousand-fold. If you were to become a spiritual giant, the problems you now regard as matters of life and death would seem very easy to solve.

When you find yourself facing a huge problem, another important key is to imagine how a great person would approach it. For instance, if you are a Christian, you may think how Jesus Christ would see your problem and go about solving it. Suppose you find yourself trapped in suffering because you find it impossible to forgive someone; just by thinking about the person, you become full of resentment and cannot sleep at night. If this happens, you should try to change your perspective and imagine what Jesus Christ would do or what advice he would give you.

If you are a Buddhist, you might ask yourself what Shakyamuni Buddha would say about your problem and how he would solve it. Or you could imagine what Confucius would do in your position or what Socrates would do. This is a very useful method to adopt when viewing problems. When making decisions and dealing with difficulties, you should refer to the wisdom of great figures.

This is quite common in companies, too. An entry-level employee may not be able to solve a certain problem, but a section manager can somehow figure out and find a solution for it. A department head will make a more sophisticated decision. An executive will make an even more outstanding decision, and the president will make the final decision. In this way, those in higher positions can make more advanced decisions.

To create a strong sense of stability, you need to develop a higher level of inner strength and accumulate spiritual wisdom. This is where the source of stability lies. If you wish to become a spiritual giant, just facing and grappling with the problems you encounter in your life is not enough; it is also essential that you extract lessons from them.

The lessons you gain in this way will stand you in good stead later. A problem you had difficulty solving the first time will become very easy to solve the next time you encounter it because you have managed to overcome it before. In order to do this, you shouldn't spend your time aimlessly but make an effort to learn valuable lessons from each of the incidents and problems you face daily. These lessons are what you need to learn in life, and they form the foundations of a precious wisdom that is rarely taught in schools.

How many drawers of lessons have you accumulated? The quantity and quality of the lessons in those drawers are closely related to your degree of awareness and your decision-making ability. From this point of view, those who are going through many life experiences, under constant hardship, and experiencing many failures, setbacks, and problems are gaining many lessons. So, you shouldn't be spending your days aimlessly. You are given an important workbook of problems to solve, so times of trial like this are actually a blessing.

When you are faced with a problem and you find yourself in a whirlpool of suffering, you shouldn't simply try to get out of it. Instead, find out what the problem is trying to teach you and what kind of lessons it is providing you with. Doing so will lead you to solve your problems. Everything has a meaning, and it is your job to find out what it is.

# 5

## Maintaining Your Strong Will

I would like to finish this chapter by talking about the importance of maintaining your strong will. In the previous section, I explained what the foundations of stability are, but this stability should not just be temporary. If you consistently aim to progress on a daily basis, this in itself produces a great sense of stability.

Take an Antarctic icebreaker, for example. As long as it keeps moving forward, it will smash its way through the ice, but once it stops, the ice will build up around it and entrap it. The same is true in life; to avoid being entrapped, you must keep moving forward. Grow every day through your experiences, and always keep in mind that with every new life lesson you learn, you become spiritually stronger and healthier.

Your stability shouldn't just be something to get by the situation. You need the kind of stability that will lead you to find solutions to any problem you may face. To do this, you must never give up on making progress and improving yourself. It's important to have a strong will like this. For those who always aspire to develop, improve, and advance, life's worries are something that will eventually disappear like dew in the morning sun. The dew will soon evaporate as the sun rises. First, let the sun within you rise high. Always make tireless efforts to let the sun rise within you. Then, a grand path will open up before you.

Ultimately, what is essential in life is for you to constantly build the foundations, continue to grow, become a bigger person, and possess the graceful stability of an iceberg. Always build your foundations and grow—never let go of this attitude, and a path to boundless development and greatness of character will open up before you.

# CHAPTER TWO

# The Principle of Accumulation

# 1

# The Significance of a Single Day

In this chapter, I would like to discuss how important it is to accumulate life's lessons to create the stability of an iceberg in your life.

First of all, I would like to consider the significance of a single day. Life is actually nothing more than a series or accumulation of single days. From ancient times, there have been various sayings about this, such as "Live each day as if it were your last," or as Jesus Christ said, "Each day has enough trouble of its own."

Put simply, the kind of person you are and the kind of life you have led are determined by the way you have lived each day and how each day has followed from the one before. Human beings can use neither tomorrow's time nor yesterday's time. You can predict what will happen in the future, but you cannot make use of time that has yet to come. In the same way, although you can reflect on what happened in the past and learn lessons from it, you cannot change the past. The only time you can freely use is the present.

Because of this, each day holds an important key to your life. Sooner or later, everyone will leave this world; some will go to heaven and some will go to hell, and it is the accumulation of your days on earth that determines where you will go. The sum total of the way you have lived each day will determine what kind of world you will go to after death, so you should be careful not to treat even a single day lightly.

As for the way you should spend each day, the important point is how you control and increase the quality of each day. You cannot change the length of a day; each one lasts for 24 hours, and there is no way this time can be extended. However, it is possible for you to change the quality of each day.

In a sense, scientific technology has been of great service in improving the quality of our days. For instance, calculations that used to take several days can now be done in a relatively short time using computers. As far as technology has shortened time, we can say we have succeeded in increasing the quality of each day. You cannot deny that technological advances have resulted in more efficient use of time.

However, it is also possible to alter the quality of each day by means of our spiritual perspective and our state of mind. The majority of people spend their lives with some kind of worry or emotional pain, and the way they deal with it will affect their whole life. It is possible for people who have a higher level of awareness to "slay" their worries or suffering in a single stroke. For example, if you devote yourself to spiritual refinement every day while keeping your mind calm, you won't be overly affected by the outside world, no matter what may happen. You will be able to lead your life with a tranquil mind with no attachments, in the same way that a river flows or the clouds drift across the sky.

On the other hand, if you are caught up in the whirlpool of a busy life, you may, at times, be seized by worries that cause you to lose yourself. For example, those who deal with the stock market may sometimes become deluded and think that following the share price every day, every hour, or even every minute is all that matters. As a result, they experience great pain if their stocks plunge in value. In contrast, however, seekers of Truth meditate calmly. This difference arises from their state of mind.

In the workplace, you may suffer from various things, such as your colleague being promoted ahead of you, being told off by your boss for your mistakes, or not making as much profit as you expected. However, these are by no means serious problems for those who have a purer mind. A problem that occupies most of your thoughts during the day can easily be settled if you look at it from a higher point of view. If you have been worrying for a week or a month about a problem that someone with a higher perspective could solve in just three minutes, it means you are accumulating a negative balance in your life.

Each day is very precious. Please give more thought to the state of mind you should have throughout the day. You cannot increase the length of a day, but you can improve or change its quality. Therefore, I would like you to think about how much and what kind of effort you need to make to change the quality of each day. Try to find the magic that changes life into gold. Try to find a way to make each day shine brightly.

# 2

## A Willingness to Learn

When considering the significance of a single day, you should examine how to improve the quality of the limited time it contains. What is important here is the aspiration to learn.

First, you can learn by gaining knowledge. As I explained in the last chapter, some of the keys to understanding life can be found in the thoughts of great figures. By reading their books of philosophy and literature, your mind will be lifted to a higher state, which will enable you to solve problems in your life quite easily. Accumulating knowledge is most important when trying to attain a higher level of awareness. Why do you need a higher level of awareness? This is because gaining higher awareness means attaining a higher spiritual grade.

In short, the greatness of a human being is determined by his or her level of awareness. It is about being able to view others and this world from a higher and broader perspective. For instance, let's say you come across something new that you need someone to teach you to understand. You will be able to grasp it more easily if you have accumulated various types of information and knowledge about the subject beforehand.

Also, misunderstandings are inevitable in life. Usually, the cause lies in not being able to understand other people's feelings or why you are confronted with certain situations. Even then, it takes time to ask each person to explain how they feel, and there could also be bad timing.

On the other hand, if you know about the lives and views of many different people, you will be able to understand why you find yourself in certain difficult situations. Accumulating knowledge will serve you greatly in understanding yourself, understanding others, and understanding this world—a world created by God.

Now, what will you acquire by gaining a better understanding of yourself, others, and the world? The answer is a sense of happiness. Knowing is a joy in itself. As you widen your sphere of understanding, your inner world, too, will become more vast.

For example, I'm sure that no one would want to be an ant. Why not? It all boils down to the worldview. There is a big difference between the worldview of an ant and that of a human being. Ants cannot think or understand in the same way that human beings can. Because of this huge gap in awareness, a human being wants to remain human and has no wish to become an ant. So knowing, in and of itself, is also a source of great happiness.

Acquiring knowledge is not the only means of learning; you can also learn from experience. To do this, you need to live each day believing that it contains something that will enrich your life. When you are in the middle of life's storm, you tend to complain and ask why you should have to suffer such pain or misfortune. But the fact is, there are certain lessons to be learned from these circumstances. There is no doubt that they work as whetstones in life with which to refine yourself.

You may want to live a calm life and hope that every day passes peacefully, but imagine when you come to the end of your life and look back over your entire life. If it was an ordinary and uneventful life, would you be able to say that you had a good life and leave this world fulfilled? In actual fact, it is when you are struggling to overcome difficulties that your soul shines and your joy increases. You will certainly experience tough times when you struggle with hardships and difficulties, but in these circumstances, you can find the richness of life and grow into a greater person.

I have no intention of regarding difficulties or distress as a wonderful thing, but it is an undeniable fact that these challenges work as catalysts for human growth. If you live a mere ordinary life, you will have no chance to grow. On the other hand, if you feel you are being torn apart by suffering, you will gain tremendous self-confidence by overcoming your struggles.

The secret of people who others see as "wise" lies in their positive attitude. They try to learn and absorb as much as possible from every person and every experience. There are countless people in this world with abilities that are better than those of the greatest saints. Confucius was undoubtedly a great man, but some people have marvelous expertise that Confucius never had. There are even things to be learned from sinful people. For example, some sinful people are caring and helpful to others.

Life is an assignment given by God or Buddha. It is about how much we can learn from our experiences. The more changes or ups and downs we experience in life, the more lessons we can learn. Our challenge is to see how much we can learn and discover from those lessons.

To conclude this section, I would like to emphasize that you should become more and more eager to learn and be proud of how much you have learned in a single day. It is fine to keep a diary, but it should not just be a report of what happened during the day. What did you learn today? That is what is important. Finding positive meaning in suffering or worries is more valuable to the soul than simply passing each day without accumulating any experiences. Nothing in life is a waste if it is seen from the perspective that all experiences are nourishment for the soul.

# 3

## The Effects of Accumulation

So far, I have discussed the significance of a single day and the importance of having a willingness to learn. Now, I would like to talk about the effects of accumulation.

In the last 10 years or so, I have published more than 300 books, and a lot of people have been surprised at how I have written so many books in such a short period of time. Without sufficient inner stock, most people would run out of ideas long before they could write such a large number of books. In my case, however, the fountain of knowledge doesn't dry out. Why? Because I take in more than I put out. In other words, I "charge" myself more than I "discharge." Some people constantly expend energy and rarely recharge themselves. But they need to understand the principle that people cannot give out more than they have in stock. For this reason, it is very important to increase your stock of knowledge and experience. You must uphold this way of thinking.

This applies not only mentally and intellectually but also financially. When it comes to family finances, you cannot spend more than you earn unless you have savings. This is why those who are wise spend within the limits of their income and save part of it. This is a sensible way of living.

Today, people use credit cards, and many bask in the benefits of our "credit card society." It seems that a lot of people enjoy living on credit, easily purchasing electrical appliances or cars that they would find difficult to buy with cash. I admit that these cards are useful, but you should not base your life on loans. The idea of using money in advance, in anticipation of future income, is a negative or hellish way of thinking that does not always accord with Buddha's Truth. God or Buddha appreciates a steady way of life, where you live within your income and accumulate savings.

In the United States, it seems that those who cannot control their spending are campaigning against credit cards. I have heard there are even people who make a living out of cutting credit cards into little pieces and throwing them away for those who cannot do it by themselves. Some people own a number of different credit cards and overuse them. Then, they find themselves deeply in debt and take out new loans to pay off the previous ones. As a result, the total amount of money they have borrowed grows larger and larger. Even then, they still cannot get rid of their credit cards. That is why they get others to destroy them so they can finally get out of the "hell of debt." This is an example of human weakness. I would like you to keep living within the limits of your income and set aside savings for the future.

The same principles apply to human souls. People tend to want to be superior to those around them, so they strive for titles and positions even when they do not have the necessary skills or abilities. This attitude is wrong because guiding people before you have accumulated sufficient abilities is the same as spending your bonus in advance and charging purchases to your credit card.

Even if everyone wished they could be the president of a company, not everyone should hold such a position. If someone who has accumulated sufficient skills and experience becomes president, he or she can bring benefits to many people. On the other hand, if someone who has no store of skills or experience becomes president, he or she will not do a good job and, as a result, will cause suffering to many people. The same holds true for actors and sports players whose popularity exceeds their abilities. It is good to achieve a level of popularity appropriate to your ability, but if your popularity is overrated, it is meaningless. Your fame and popularity should follow your ability. If you try to win popularity beyond your level of competence, you will lose your footing.

Therefore, to be victorious in life, you must accumulate knowledge and experience. Even if the skills you accumulate are not used or appreciated in this lifetime, they will be stored as wealth in heaven. Some things you learn in this life may not help you at work or in your family life. However, nothing you learn will ever go to waste. You may have studied physics, chemistry, or geography in school and wondered how they will help you in the future, but they will all serve as material for gaining a well-balanced understanding of things in life.

This phenomenon can be called the "usefulness of the useless." It means that something that seems useless can actually be useful. No matter how large a bridge may be, it only needs to be about a foot wide for a person to be able to walk across it. However, this is not to say that the rest of the bridge is useless. Suppose there was a log bridge one foot wide over a quick-flowing stream; most people would be afraid of the rapid stream beneath them, unable to cross. Similarly, anyone can walk along a rope on the ground, but you will be impressed and amazed when someone walks on a tightrope bridging two roofs.

In this way, many things may be unnecessary, but thanks to them, you are protected from various dangers and can keep a stable mind. This is what I mean by the usefulness of the useless. It is this inner accumulation that constitutes your true ability. If you have not accumulated much, you are likely to be swayed by small things, whereas if you have accumulated a great deal within and have absolute self-confidence, you will not be easily swayed by unfavorable criticism or setbacks. For this reason, it is important to accumulate sufficient knowledge and experience, which will together become like the submerged part of an iceberg.

Inner accumulation has another surprising effect; it will unexpectedly provide the key to opening up your life. Even if your store of knowledge does not seem to be of any use now, in 10 or 20 years, it may bloom in a way that you could never have imagined. It is not easy to know what you will need in the future. Although you may feel that many of your experiences have been unnecessary, perhaps they will serve you in times to come.

As for myself, before I entered the path of religion, I worked for six years in a general trading company. While I was working there, the question always arose, "Why should I spend most of my time each day working in a field that has nothing to do with Buddha's Truth or matters of the mind?" Again and again, the thought crossed my mind that this work could not be what I was born to do. My job in the company was dealing with foreign exchange, international finance, and domestic funds, so I had a good understanding of the way money flowed. At the same time, I thought the financial field had nothing to do with the world of the mind, and I had a vague sense of anxiety about the direction my life was taking.

However, I realize now that those experiences have stood me in good stead at Happy Science. During my time at the trading company, I learned about people, how to manage an organization, how money flows, how to make efficient use of funds, etc., and all these things have been useful in my current work.

Many of those who intend to accomplish something in the spiritual arena seem to lack the skills of organizational management and putting money to good use. Many religious leaders, in particular, are ignorant of these sorts of practical matters. Lacking knowledge and experience, they fail to manage their groups and ultimately fail to accomplish their main purpose or fulfill their original intention. However, because I made the utmost effort in fields that seemed to have nothing to do with the Truth, in other words, because I accumulated what seemed unnecessary, I have an inner store of knowledge and experience. I actually feel that this now helps me in different ways.

During my time at the trading company, I also had the chance to work in the United States with people from all over the world, not only Americans but also Koreans, Chinese, Filipinos, and such. This experience gave me the opportunity to get to know the ways of thinking and characteristics of people from various countries. I got to know values that were different from my own.

Today, I teach the diversity of the Truth and the diversity of what is right. I can say that this teaching originates from my experiences in international society, where lots of different people with various ways of thinking taught me valuable lessons. I learned that there are numerous ways of thinking besides my own that are reasonable, and this helped me develop a diverse way of thinking. There are many religious leaders with different teachings, yet they all insist that their particular teaching is everything. But I do not think like this because I have worked with people of many different nationalities and races and fully absorbed their ways of thinking. The way this has helped me is an example of the usefulness of the useless.

Therefore, people's abilities and character are polished through their work. Even if you are now engaged in something that seems far from useful in terms of your future aims, in time, what you have learned will serve you in some way. You may feel that you are doing something irrelevant or that you are taking the long way around in reaching your aim or ideal, but it is important to make the best use of the materials you are being given now.

If you keep on solving the problems you are presented with, in due course, this will serve you in some way. Even if you feel that the mathematics you studied at school has been of very little use to you since you graduated, the learning you have undergone serves to provide a sense of balance for your character and your knowledge. To use another example, it is not enough for a novelist to just read works of literature. A writer needs to know about the world and the changes taking place in society to support his or her work.

In order to accumulate knowledge and experience, you must not limit your studies to what you need to know right now. Rather, you should take an interest in a wide range of subjects and continue gathering information. Even if it is not useful to you right now, accumulating knowledge that you feel may become useful in the future will have a great effect on you someday.

# 4

## An Unexpected Harvest

In the previous section, I explained that as a result of accumulating knowledge and experience, you will reap an unexpected harvest. Sometimes it happens in this lifetime, sometimes in the next. It is not unusual to find people who seemed quite miserable in this world achieve a wonderful state after death in the other world. It also happens that people who were nameless in this world reach a surprisingly high level in the other world.

Mary, who gave birth to Jesus, was not very cultured but had a pure heart and lived an ordinary life as a carpenter's wife. She could barely see Jesus as a savior and loved him simply as her own son. When Jesus reached the age of 30, he started teaching people about God. Many people became his followers, but he was also persecuted. Mary just wanted happiness for her beloved son. That is what she wished for all through her life. On witnessing Jesus' crucifixion, she cried and screamed as if she had lost her mind. Mary was such a kind of person. She never thought of herself as someone special. However, long after leaving this world and returning to the Real World, she is now known as the Virgin Mary, one of the most revered women in the world. When Mary returned to the heavenly world, she was confused and surprised about all kinds of things for a while, but she eventually returned to her original position. She has returned to her brilliant self as a high spirit worthy of being called the Virgin Mary.

Now, she listens to the worries of many and works hard for the sake of people all over the world, especially women, children, and families. In this earthly world, Mary lived an ordinary life, the life of a carpenter's wife. But it was a life in line with the Truth. She never expected to become someone special after death. She treated her husband, children, and neighbors with great kindness and lived with faith. She was not concerned with worldly status, fame, or honor, and it is an undeniable fact that she loved her son, Jesus, with her whole heart. People like her reap as much harvest as they deserve after leaving this world. It is said, "Even if you do not seek divine favor, it will be given to you." I believe these words express this piece of Truth about the heavenly world well.

Although you need to accumulate different experiences in life and build up an inner store, you should not be doing so just to seek good outcomes. Do not be too concerned with the results. Life is full of unexpected harvests and sudden reversals. It is possible even for someone such as a respected prime minister or president to fall to hell, while someone who has led an ordinary life could go to a brilliant world. The criteria that determine where you will go after death are the purity of your mind and how sincere and selfless you are.

Those who possess these traits see everything as material for learning, leading them along a path of self-development.

To reap an unexpected harvest, you must tirelessly strive to live a sincere life with a pure heart. When you live sincerely, you may sometimes be misunderstood or laughed at in this world. However, your attitude of being committed to living sincerely with a pure heart will definitely yield an abundant harvest at some point. For example, I have been revealing the Truth about the world of the mind and the reality of the Spirit World in many of my books. But not everyone can understand these things. Some people misunderstand them. However, I tell myself to keep moving forward as long as I can vow from the bottom of my heart that I do not speak lies but speak with a pure heart. I believe it is important to preach the Truth as it is. People will understand me eventually.

Now, I am filled with the determination to publish as many books of Truth and about the mind as possible. Be it a small number of people, I hope my books will help people open up their new life. I will be happy if these books help people find happiness and nourishment for their souls, not only for the people living in this current generation but also for those who will be born after I leave this world. This is my wish.

You should not accumulate knowledge and experience for the purpose of fulfilling selfish desires or satisfying your own interests. It is essential to accumulate wisdom day by day, with a pure wish to be of service to the Great One in times to come. This is the true meaning of "storing up treasures in heaven." Do not seek the approval of others in this world or the next. It is important to live with a pure heart and tell people what you believe. You must never leave things as they are if you know you will regret it later.

# 5

# The Path to Reproducing Happiness

I would like to finish this chapter by discussing the path to reproducing happiness. Human beings gain many different types of knowledge in the course of their lives; they also learn a lot of lessons from their numerous experiences. This learning is not just for themselves, nor is it simply for the sake of gaining knowledge. For example, the money you earn through working will be worth nothing if you simply leave it unused. It only has meaning when you use it. When you use money, you circulate it so that what you earn becomes others' income.

The same can be said of experiences. What you experience or realize from events in your life should not just be for your own satisfaction. It is important for you to produce something that enlightens others from what you have learned. In your lifetime, you will probably learn many lessons. Instead of storing these lessons up just for yourself, you should pass them on to society in different forms. You can share them with your family, with your friends, and with the many people you encounter in your life.

You first need to attain a higher level of enlightenment day by day. Then, you will be able to lead others to a higher enlightenment using your own stock of learning. What is more, you shouldn't only give your enlightenment to others in an obvious way. You should be aware that the very existence of a person who has acquired much knowledge, learned lessons, and attained a higher level of enlightenment is an expression of great love for others. This is one form of *love incarnate** that I teach. If there is even a single person in a company who has attained a high level of enlightenment through learning life's lessons, he or she will be a great source of love to those who work in that company. Imagine what great love this person brings as an embodiment of love incarnate.

For those who seek Dharma or the Truth, how blessed are they to have such a teacher! This is something money cannot buy. The existence of Buddha, Jesus, Confucius, and Socrates was invaluable to those who were living in the same age as them. The Chinese Buddhist monk T'ien-t'ai Chih-i (538-597) said, "I wish to be reborn at the time of the rebirth of Buddha. I would not even mind being a leper as long as I could be alive then." What he said is very true. The very existence of someone who has attained great enlightenment and become a great teacher brings happiness to those who are living in the same time period.

Not everyone is able to preach the Dharma, but even you, as small as a bean, are capable of emitting the light of enlightenment. Everyone has the potential to become love incarnate in their own small circle.

*Refer to *The Laws of the Sun* (New York: IRH Press, 2018)

Rather than just simply accumulating experiences and knowledge you gained in the course of your life, you should also use what you have accumulated for the joy and happiness of others. Once you have attained happiness, reproduce it for the benefit of others. This is the duty of human beings. Please visualize yourself reproducing happiness in your heart and strive to accumulate inner resources.

# CHAPTER THREE

# Confronting Distress in Life

# 1

## Various Types of Distress in Life

When considering how to live happily, everything comes back to how you confront distress or the adversities that you face in the course of your life. Life is like a workbook of problems to be solved, and each person is given challenges that are appropriate for their soul. It is the way in which you overcome these trials that determines your true value. The suffering you experience in life clearly shows what kind of spiritual training you are going through and what is most valuable for you.

The word "adversity" makes me think of the composer, Beethoven. Imagine the adversities he must have gone through while continuing to compose music as he was losing his hearing. No one would want a life as difficult as Beethoven's, but he was a man who always gave his utmost and whose soul undoubtedly shone.

A more recent example is Helen Keller. It would be difficult to say who is greater if we compare Helen Keller with Napoleon Bonaparte or Johann Wolfgang von Goethe. Although Napoleon was a hero, he probably only had a few nights where he could sleep peacefully. Similarly, the great writer and statesman Goethe seemed to have had many sleepless nights. He once said, "The days where I truly felt happy in my life would not even add up to a month."

Why is Helen Keller's life considered as admirable as the lives of these great figures? I would say it is because of her attitude; despite the great adversities she suffered, she made a constant effort to find the wonder in everything. When people are healthy and their lives flow smoothly, they have a tendency to focus on what is lacking. However, if they were to find themselves unable to see, hear, or speak, all they have left is the fact they are alive. People must realize that just being alive is wonderful.

I have heard that sometimes, people who have lost their sight dream only in sounds and darkness. But they are still alive, and even in such adverse circumstances, they are able to grasp the true meaning of life. From time to time, you need to look at yourself and learn from the examples of those who have lived through great hardship.

What is the cause of your suffering or distress? Quite often, it comes from something trivial. In most cases, your suffering comes from emotional conflict. I think many of you are creating suffering as a result of trying to find the balance between how you feel and how others feel. The cause of most suffering is a conflict with others. However, you will never be able to free yourself of suffering as long as you compare yourself with others. That is because if you look back at your past or look around you, there will always be someone you envy. This is true for everyone.

In ancient Greece, there was a philosopher named Diogenes. It is said that he always dressed in rags and lived in a large tub; he was known as "the sage in the tub." One day, Alexander the Great visited the town, and upon meeting Diogenes, he announced, "Tell me what you desire, and I will grant your wish." However, Diogenes merely said, "Please stand out of the way; you're blocking the sunlight." This story has been handed down for over 2,000 years.

Happiness for Diogenes was a quiet life, basking in the sun in his tub. He enjoyed peace of mind and needed nothing more than that. He was satisfied with just bathing in the sun; he never had the slightest desire for fine clothes or money, status, fame, or anything else. All he wanted was to sit in his tub and think; he just wanted to be free to do exactly as he wished without anyone else telling him what to do. Then came Alexander the Great, in whom Diogenes did not have the slightest interest, and stood in front of him, blocking the sunlight. That is why Diogenes said, "Please move out of the way." The king was left speechless.

Alexander believed that there was nothing in the world that was not under his dominion. Certainly, he had the power to fulfill any worldly desire; he could grant any wish for a palace, money, or a wife. Yet, despite possessing such powers, Alexander the Great was nothing more than an obstruction to Diogenes, blocking the sunlight and casting a shadow over him. This episode illustrates the difference between someone who inhabits the kingdom within and someone who lives for the glory of the material world.

There is a similar anecdote from ancient China. Chuang-tzu (367-279 B.C.), one of the most famous Chinese philosophers during the period of the Hundred Schools of Thought, had a similar experience. When he was offered a post as a minister, he turned it down instantly. The story goes that he said he would rather frolic in the mud like a pig than live a suffocating life of service. Worldly status meant absolutely nothing to him.

In the replies of these two men, I see figures who were perfect sovereigns in their own kingdom of the mind and unswayed by the circumstances around them or by worldly standards. One man was happy without wanting any of the power, fame, or money that Alexander the Great could give; the other wanted to frolic in the mud like a pig rather than hold a ministerial post. Neither of these men allowed their happiness to be influenced by the words or opinions of others or by circumstances others had created; they were great men because they were rulers of their own kingdom within.

When I look at the different types of distress people have, I see that the cause of their suffering lies in the fact that they are trying to fit into the standards of others, that they are swayed by the words of others, and that they struggle to stay independent and have their own opinions. People are distressed because all kinds of information enters their eyes and ears. Therefore, it all comes down to you comparing yourself with others. This is the cause of your suffering.

From time to time, remind yourself of the stories of the two men. View your suffering again from the perspective that maybe you are trying to attain happiness by imposing outside values on your inner world. You should ask yourself, "Is it just that I'm not yet in complete control of the kingdom of my mind? Compared to them, am I still a weak human who is swayed easily by mere status, money, or the opposite sex? Am I seeking my happiness and unhappiness on outside factors? Is that why I'm suffering?"

# 2
# Anxiety in Life

The origins of most anxieties in life are to be found in a person's sense of value. Anxiety usually stems from a fear of being regarded as inferior to how you wish to be seen or losing your value. For instance, when you fall in love with someone, you may be scared of being rejected by him or her; when you start working for a company, you may be worried that you will never be promoted to a high position; when you launch a business, you may be afraid that it will go bankrupt. Or you may be scared of falling sick. Such anxieties all stem from being worried that things will be worse for you than they are now. So, the fundamental cause of distress or anxiety in life is the belief that your happiness depends on outside factors. This way of thinking shakes and destabilizes your mind.

Now, I would like to talk about the story of Job from the Old Testament. Job, a good and righteous man, had strong faith; no matter what happened, his faith never wavered. However, there was a time when Job suffered from a series of misfortunes. Many of his cattle died, his servants were murdered, and his sons and daughters died in accidents. As if that wasn't enough, he developed boils all over his body and became utterly miserable. In this way, Job lost everything he had, including his health.

At that moment, Job shouted to heaven, "O God, I have been living righteously with faith, so why am I met with these misfortunes? Is this not a mistake? Those who live with deep faith deserve to be blessed with happy circumstances; they should be rewarded with success, prosperity, and glory accordingly. So why does misfortune after misfortune befall me? My whole family is wretched. I have lost many of my cattle. I, myself, have become hideous. Why do I have to suffer in this way?"

God then replied, "O Job, what do you know about heaven and God? Do you understand the Will of God? Do you understand the true thoughts of the One who created this universe? Don't you understand why I am giving you these ordeals? You are cursing your environment, but this thinking, in itself, is where you are mistaken."

In short, what the Old Testament is trying to teach here is that you will not attain happiness by cursing your environment; true faith does not mean believing in God when things are going well for you but not when they are not. Faith is an internal matter within you. Faith does not allow external factors to intrude upon it. What is important is that you protect your kingdom within, even if you are crucified, shot by bullets, or crushed by a tank. You may be criticized or verbally abused by others, which may be like being shot by bullets. However, you need to have an unshakable belief, a faith that will not sway even under gunfire.

When everything was going well, Job believed earnestly in God. However, when he was beset by misfortune, he suddenly began to lose faith. You can see numerous examples of this in daily life. For instance, you may trust someone who has treated you well, but as soon as your situation changes for the worse, you lose trust in that person.

The same thing can happen in a company. As long as your boss treats you well, you may work hard for him, but the moment he stops favoring you, you may criticize him. This is the behavior of an average person. The same thing also happens in religious groups. People work hard when they are given an important role, but as soon as they are relieved of their role, they start to complain. This attitude is the height of folly.

These people are in the same position as Job. It is not difficult for them to live rightly and with faith when their circumstances are favorable. It is in times of deep adversity that their faith is tested. Sometimes, God or Buddha sends human beings ordeals to temper their souls. The soul is strengthened in both the times of good fortune and times of adversity, and it is through these two extremes that your true nature is revealed. God or Buddha demands human beings to not become conceited in good times and to not fall into deep despair in times of misfortune. Rather, He expects us to keep making steady efforts in every situation.

All anxiety in life originates from the concern that your standing will drop in comparison to others. You begin to question whether what you thought was your strength is truly your strength. Suppose a woman feels that her beauty is the sole source of her happiness. What will she be left with when her beauty fades? What about a man who regards his youth as the only quality he values in himself? What will happen to him when he is no longer young?

Here, I am trying to illustrate the true nature of anxiety. You writhe in agony, unable to endure situations when something external could hurt you or reduce your worth. At these times, you need to be aware that your faith and conviction are being tested. If you only believe in God when everything is going well and do not believe in Him in unfavorable situations, it means that your faith is not real and that you are only looking for the advantages that faith can bring.

So please understand that most anxieties in life stem from believing that the seed of your happiness is found in the world outside of you. Anxieties arise because you have not yet established a firm inner self and you have not yet taken full responsibility for your mind.

# 3

# On Sleepless Nights

Most people have probably experienced sleepless nights as their mind wavered in distress amid life's worries. Some of you may be having restless nights at the moment. You lie awake in bed and gaze into the darkness, unable to get a wink of sleep as you wait for dawn. When you are finally on the verge of dozing off, it becomes time to get up. You have to go to work, but you are not feeling well, are in a bad mood, and feel distinctly unhappy. You have probably experienced a night like this.

How can you cope with sleepless nights? Usually, loss of sleep comes from worry. For those who suffer from sleepless nights, I would like to point out some facts. First, sleepless nights do not continue for very long. No one ever has difficulty sleeping for as long as three or four years; it is only temporary. Another fact is that your soul is being tempered. What is important during these times is how much you can polish, forge, and temper your soul. This is how you must think.

If you continue to have sleepless nights, you need to endure this time instead of making any hasty decisions about what to do. According to the Japanese statesman Kaishu Katsu (1823-1899), life cycles alternate every seven to ten years, so if you stand in the shade for 10 years, you will eventually see the sun again. On the other hand, although the sun may be shining on you now, in another 10 years, you may experience the shade. He says that the tides of destiny do not flow in the same direction for more than 10 years. This is quite possible. Just because the sun is not shining on you now, there is very little to be gained by wailing, lamenting, and complaining about it. People are calmly watching to see how you lead your life in the face of adversity. If you behave in the same way that people who suffer misfortune usually do, you will learn nothing from the experience, and as a result, others will not hold you in very high regard.

How you lead your life when you are going through adversity is very important. If we were to classify human beings into top, middle, and lower levels, those who moan, complain, or get angry in times of misfortune belong at the lowest level. Those who quietly endure sorrow or pain belong in the middle. Those who try to get over their pain and better themselves are a bit above the middle. Those who think that adversity is precisely the time they must do their best belong to the top level.

Now, how do those who belong at the high end of the top deal with adversities? These people will try to find positive meaning in difficult situations and learn lessons to further strengthen their souls. You must train yourself to be strong instead of holding on to misfortune for a long time. This is essential.

Once, I read a story about a child who had a weak body and was told he would not grow up to be healthy if he stayed the way he was. So, he decided to overcome his physical condition and trained himself by running along a river bank. In the end, he became an Olympic athlete who represented his country. Contrary to what you may think, this is how life works. Even if you think you are below average, if you stay composed and continue to work on yourself with peace of mind instead of complaining or merely enduring your lack of ability, you will leap to unexpected heights.

Some people hold on to the fact that they are unhappy; they try to get out of their unhappiness and improve their lives while holding on to their misfortune. On the other hand, some continue to strengthen and improve themselves calmly and collectedly every day, without much concern for their misfortune. The difference between the two is vast.

On sleepless nights, you should concentrate on making efforts to improve yourself. If you cannot sleep, it simply means you have more time to do other things. When I had sleepless nights, I did not force myself to sleep; instead, I focused my energy on reading. It definitely won't be a waste to spend time developing and improving yourself when you are in the midst of difficulties, worries, or anxieties. If I had been an athlete, perhaps I would have trained my body by running marathons. However, I was not an athlete. My interest was in the world of the mind and the world of thoughts, so I trained myself by studying in those areas.

I began communicating with the Spirit World when I was 24 years old, yet it was not until I was 30 that I stood up and began to teach Buddha's Truth. For six years, I quietly continued developing my inner strength, waiting for the right time to come. During that period, I could have worried endlessly had I wanted to because although I was experiencing spiritual phenomena and had been told a clear mission to carry out, a suitable environment had not manifested around me, and I could not start out on my new path. However, I did not spend my time worrying; instead, I led a busy life. I was determined to work harder than anyone else and to create an above-average record at my company, while at the same time, I was dedicating all my time outside of work to investing in my future.

I am now engaged in my true mission, and looking back at my past, I feel proud of my attitude and the fact that I concentrated on developing myself rather than struggling in vain. If, at that time, I had spent my days worrying about how my situation had not changed despite receiving revelations from high spirits and realizing my grand mission, I may not be who I am today. Instead, during that time, I thought about my future. "What do I need to do? In the near future, I will have to give talks in front of large numbers of people and write books. In order to do that, it will be essential to have refined myself spiritually and to have a store of knowledge. It will take four, five, maybe six decades to learn the many lessons I need through experience, so I must back up my lack of experience with knowledge." With this thinking, I concentrated on developing myself. I had no doubt that sooner or later, the appropriate circumstances would be given to me, so I just kept on developing myself further without worrying.

This is one way of coping with sleepless nights. Instead of complaining that you have not been provided with the circumstances you need for your mission, you should tell yourself that if you really have a mission, the appropriate circumstances will be given to you at the appropriate time, and you will blossom according to your potential. You have no way of knowing when this will be; until then, you should work to improve yourself tirelessly, focusing on what you think will be required of you. Without self-pity or sadness, you should build up your strength. Those who are easily swayed when they face difficulties are nothing but ordinary people. At such times, you should make ceaseless and diligent efforts.

# 4

# The Sun Will Rise Again

The expression "the sun will rise again" may be an old, overused phrase, but it describes one of life's truths; there is no doubt that the sun will rise again. Every evening, the sun disappears below the horizon and surely rises again after about 10 hours of darkness. The sun promises that even though it will sink, it will certainly rise again.

I wonder if there is anyone in the whole world who thinks the sun will not come up. I am sure everyone believes that the sun will rise again; no one ever doubts it. Why is this so? It is because the sun came up this morning, yesterday morning, the day before yesterday, and last year, too. It rose 10 years ago and even when our ancestors were living, so there is no reason to doubt that it will come up tomorrow and the day after. The same holds true in life. No matter what hardship or difficulty you may face, the sun will rise again.

When you are experiencing difficulty or suffering, I strongly recommend that you look calmly at yourself from the perspective of a third person and consider whether or not anyone else has ever faced the same problem. Although people tend to think that their own worries are huge and there is nothing they can do to solve them, most problems are not unique. Similar problems have usually occurred in the past, and they are occurring now as well. In most cases, other people have experienced distress or suffering similar to yours.

Let me tell you an interesting fact that relates to this. There are people with serious illnesses who are proud to be suffering from them. If they go to the doctor and are told that it is nothing to worry about, they are not satisfied with the diagnosis and will go to another doctor. If they are told the same thing again, they will go on to the next doctor. Only when they have been told that their condition is very serious are they finally satisfied. There are numerous patients like this, and surprisingly, many people are relieved to be told their illness is unique.

Although not so common in Japan, quite a number of cases like this have been reported in Western psychiatry. Instead of trying to overcome their illness, many patients argue with their doctor, seeking to be diagnosed with complications. Cases like these happen often, and they are giving psychiatrists a lot of trouble. In other words, when someone who wants to feel superior to others experiences difficulties, they take incidents like these as an opportunity to be told how special they are. That is why they are causing trouble for psychiatrists, wanting to be told they are such complex and sensitive people. I am sure similar sorts of issues occur in relationships other than a psychiatrist-patient relationship.

Therefore, I would like you to check and see whether you are trying to satisfy something within yourself by pretending to worry and suffer. Are you sure you are not trying to make yourself into a tragic hero because you are not recognized in this world? Can you honestly say that you are not pretending to suffer anxiety out of a desire to be recognized as complex and sensitive? These are the questions you need to ask yourself. There are people who always think worse about their health and other problems, but they need to end this tendency at some point in life.

Many people take secret pleasure in the idea that they are miserable and deserve pity. They complain in many different ways, for instance: "I am unhappy because of this illness," "If only I had gotten a better score in the exam, my life would be better today," "The environment I was living in at that time caused my present situation," "If only that had not happened," or "If only things had been different." This is called self-pity. Because people who pity themselves feel that others do not love them, they try hard to provide love for themselves.

By doing this, they may think they are supplying themselves with "fertilizer," but unfortunately, the fertilizer contains poison. If they keep doing it, sooner or later, the "flowers" will wither away and die. Self-pity is poisonous in the sense that it works against people's genuine spiritual growth. As long as people love themselves in a self-pitying way, they can never gain richness in their hearts nor become wonderful people. Many people have a tendency to search for the slightest excuse to drive themselves into a corner, set themselves up as tragic heroes, and then take pleasure in their wounds. These people need to be aware that self-pity never leads to true happiness.

For instance, there are people who spend as long as four or five years suffering from heartbreak. They may think that their partner was a wonderful person, and although they did everything they could for them, their love was not rewarded. They remain heartbroken for four or five years, believing there is no cure.

Although they believed that the person they loved was the most beautiful woman or the most handsome man in the world, in most cases, the object of their love appeared quite ordinary to the people close to them. Even Marilyn Monroe would have looked quite ordinary to her family and not particularly attractive. No matter how amazing stars may appear to be on TV or in movies, in their private lives, they are mostly just ordinary women wearing beautiful make-up or ordinary men who are no different from men you find anywhere else. In most cases, these "stars" do not think of themselves as extraordinary and do not have high self-esteem.

That is how humans are. People tend to idealize others on a whim, get hurt on their own, and then get caught up in self-pity. For example, you may idealize a woman, but when you carefully think about it, she is not really a one-of-a-kind or the most beautiful woman in the world. She is usually just someone that happened to be in your class at school, in your office at work, or someone you met on another occasion. She may seem ideal to you out of the small number of women you have met, but you are not necessarily seeing this woman objectively. The tragedy begins because you stubbornly believe that she is the only one.

The bottom line is that the key to letting the sun rise again is not holding on to the night for too long. You must know that the night will pass. In fact, you should part ways with self-pity as soon as possible and cast off the negative idea that this world has abandoned you. Know that you are a magnificent child of Buddha, and let this self-recognition support your life. It is essential that you keep moving forward with this awareness.

Although one person may criticize you, another will praise you. Even if you cannot tell which person's opinion is true, just keep moving forward. Only when the lid of your coffin is closed will it become clear what kind of a person you really were. Therefore, do not be upset by what others say at any moment in time. I am not telling you to live an egotistical life; I am simply saying that other people will not always understand you.

It is a fact that those who indulge in self-pity or have a tendency to be tragic heroes often find themselves in tragic environments. In the same way, those who belittle themselves often become targets of abuse. The same thing happens with dogs. People avoid hitting or throwing stones at a dog that looks strong but may abuse a dog that looks ready to run at the slightest threat. This perversity is part of human nature.

For this reason, it is important that you do not let yourself appear weak. Never indulge in self-pity; instead, walk your own path calmly and steadily. This is the secret of how to make the sun rise again.

# 5

## Take Steady Steps

I would like to finish this chapter on confronting distress in life by talking about the importance of taking steady steps. In times of adversity, your mind will sway like a leaf in the wind, and you tend to see problems as extremely serious. At such times, you must remember two perspectives.

One is the macro-perspective: to see yourself from infinitely far away. In the midst of your suffering and confusion, look at yourself through the eyes of Buddha, from His vast perspective. Think to yourself, is what is happening really so grave? In most cases, it is simply the result of comparing yourself with just a few hundred or a few thousand people, such as those at your company. You might be upset that your colleague got a bigger bonus than you or was promoted to a higher position before you. Perhaps the cause is family circumstances; maybe your wife has become ill.

It is important to ask yourself if the adversity you are facing is really so enormous or whether it is actually a small thing, a common occurrence that will pass in time. This ability to see yourself from an infinite distance is essential for solving life's problems.

The other important perspective is the micro-perspective: to focus on enriching each day. When misfortune strikes, some people start working desperately in a bid to be noticed by others. They may attempt to do something that stands out or begin to talk big. For instance, someone who is suffering from heartbreak may suddenly start something new out of an eagerness to show that he is unaffected. A person who has failed to get a promotion may suddenly start to brag about his hobbies. In this way, some people try hard to show another side of themselves out of their pain.

But in most cases, these people become filled with self-hatred and find themselves in even more pain after three to six months. So it is true that when you are going through a hard time, you should not make any moves or do anything showy. You should not do something big or brag in front of others in reaction to pain. If you do, it will bring about an even worse outcome and make you hate yourself even more.

When you are in pain, do not make any dramatic moves to attract the attention of others. Instead of acting in a showy way, keep walking steadily on your own path. It is also important to have this micro-perspective. Try to transform yourself within your own capabilities and become a better person; walk steadily along the path to self-improvement. Never mind the eyes of others, but devote yourself to developing your abilities 24 hours a day.

Some people working in companies talk big about starting a grand project. They cannot let go of their frustration for failing a project they were entrusted with previously. However, that is when you are mentally and emotionally unstable. It means your "battery" has died and needs to be recharged. To recharge it, you need to act in a moderate fashion and spend your time building up an inner store. If you fail at work, you should not embark on even bigger projects to preserve your pride. Instead, you should look at yourself calmly and cultivate your inner self for about half a year.

The most important thing is for you to walk forward and take steady steps, day by day. Make sure to take care of your health and enrich your inner self. Whenever you see something outside of you and your mind is being swayed by it, direct your mind inward to create an inner store.

Just because war has broken out in a foreign country does not mean you should run around with a spear in your hand. To build a nation that is not exposed to war, you need to educate people, construct a stable economy, and create productive agriculture. The point is that you must establish firm foundations within. Whenever you are off guard, you are liable to attacks from outside. So do not leave any openings or unguarded areas in your mind.

As I have explained, there are two main perspectives with which to confront distress. One is to view any misfortune that occurs from a macro-perspective, that is to say, from the perspective of Buddha. Then, you may become aware that your problem is not as big as you imagined or that it is a common occurrence. The problem will eventually pass by.

The other perspective is to see yourself from the microperspective. You should not talk big, plan major projects, or take dramatic action to try to justify your failure. If you do, you will be regarded as someone without much potential. When you are discouraged, you should remain serene and continue developing yourself.

If you really are an important and competent member of society, you will not be left unnoticed forever; you will eventually be recognized. I am not saying that you should wait for seven or ten years for the cycle to pass, like what Kaishu Katsu said. I assume that within six months to a year, the day will come when you are reassessed and presented with a new position. In the meantime, you should be reserved in speech and action and refine your inner self. You should walk forward steadily every day; this is one of the guiding principles for you to confront and overcome distress.

# CHAPTER FOUR

# Various Types of Evil Spirits

# 1

## About Evil Spirits

People who believe in the existence of the Spirit World may be interested in evil spirits or malicious spirits. But the reality is, although they may have heard of such spirits in folktales or horror stories, most people do not think that evil spirits have anything to do with their lives. However, in the unseen world, evil spirits are definitely working and plotting in secret. Even some of you reading this book are likely being manipulated and influenced by them.

So, what are evil spirits? The best way to describe them is that they are spirits living off the negative energy that humans emit. In other words, they live on people's negative thought energy. Those who often had negative thoughts while they were alive on earth have gone to the realm of hell after they died and now live there as evil spirits. This means that evil spirits were not originally created evil, but rather, everyone has the possibility of becoming an evil spirit.

As human beings, we have been granted the freedom to hold any kind of thought we want in our minds, and by exercising this freedom, we are able to change ourselves. By using this freedom of thought to its full extent, people can either become like angels or even devils. Evil spirits are those who have failed to use this freedom of the mind correctly.

Where did evil spirits go wrong? Let us focus on this point. People become evil spirits because they have generated harmful thoughts toward others. An attitude of loving oneself is not wrong, but it is undeniable that self-love contains feelings of either active or passive ill-will toward others. Within an egocentric mindset is the wish to bring others down or the wish to be the best at something.

If the wish to value oneself is used correctly, it can accord with the principles of development and prosperity. However, if it is misused even slightly, it will bring a great number of negative consequences. For example, if you only think of yourself, you can dump excretion or whatever you want into a river without thinking of how it will affect others. But the consequence of this is that people living downstream will be troubled.

For this reason, there are specific rules about garbage disposal. For instance, in Japan, there is a rule that you can only take your garbage to a designated place on particular days of the week. If you were only concerned about keeping the inside of your house clean, you wouldn't care about tossing your garbage onto the street. However, this is not permitted.

Those who cannot understand why this is not allowed will be labeled a troublemaker by others. Whether or not a person can understand rules like this will demonstrate his or her nature as a human being. This is because the fundamental challenge of being human lies in how to live as an individual while living in harmony with the whole of society. As an individual, each person needs to manifest his or her own uniqueness and distinctive qualities, but at the same time, the individual needs to create harmony and contribute to the development of society as a whole.

Here lies the origin of evil spirits. Evil is a distortion that arises when individuals with freedom come into conflict with one another. Evil spirits are those that embody evil in the course of their lives and live in accordance with evil.

Humans are spiritual beings and are nothing but the content of their thoughts. Evil arises when someone tries to attribute the cause of their misfortune to the environment or to other people. You should consider the correct way or a better way to live as a human being from the perspective of governing your inner self.

No matter what kind of life you are living, it is difficult to change your environment. However, you can always change what is in your mind. About 2,000 years ago, three men were crucified on a hill in Golgotha in Israel. Two of them were criminals; one was a thief, and another was a thief and a murderer. The third man was called a criminal for allegedly declaring himself to be the King of the Jews, and for this reason, he was mocked and called the "King of the Jews." He was none other than the famous Jesus Christ. They were equally crucified, but in terms of what was in their minds, there was a world of difference between the state of mind of Jesus and that of the other two men.

As this story shows, no matter what kind of situation you may be placed in, you are given complete autonomy over your mind. So, the nature of the thoughts in your mind during the course of your life is very important.

In fact, evil spirits come into being because they have failed to use the freedom they were bestowed with correctly. For example, while a fruit knife can be used to peel fruit, it can also be used to injure people. The knife does not come with instructions that it should only be used to peel fruit and not to hurt people; this is left to the conscience of the individual. In short, good and evil arise during the process of exercising our freedom, which is the most precious gift that human beings are given.

If Buddha created a mechanism to prevent humans from having negative thoughts, we would lose our freedom. This would mean that the exquisite beauty of life and the material given to us for spiritual discipline would no longer exist. Evil is allowed, from a higher perspective, as a catalyst to effectively develop our soul. Evil spirits are the pitiful result of misusing the freedom of the soul.

# 2

## Religion-Related Spirits

I would now like to talk about the different types of evil spirits. First, there are religion-related spirits. These spirits make their way into misguided religions and possess the people involved in them.

There are currently a large number of religious groups in Japan. It is said that the total number of their members would amount to hundreds of millions and surpass the entire population of Japan. Many people are associated with religious groups in one way or another. Among them are many misguided groups where evil spirits have found a way into the mind of the founder, influenced the teachings, and misled their followers. Large numbers of religion-related spirits inhabit these misguided groups. As the saying goes, "Far from Jupiter, far from his thunder," you should not get involved with these groups.

What causes this type of spirit to appear in the world? Many spirits in hell want to be saved, and they are always searching for ways to lessen their pain and distress. They are waiting for someone to eliminate their suffering and bring them relief. When hellish spirits go to a misguided religion and possess its believers, fortunately for them, those believers will realize they are possessed and start praying to "save" them. For this reason, large numbers of religion-related spirits enter misguided religions so they can have their existence recognized. These religions function as supply centers of evil spirits. Oftentimes, people who had no particular troubles before joining a misguided religion experience disharmony in their homes after they become involved and are possessed by religion-related spirits.

There are other particularly malign spirits described as devils or satans. These beings try to take over good religions and hinder the work of Bodhisattvas of Light. They are always on the lookout for opportunities to confuse the members of good religions and cause the religion to split into factions. Satans are frequently found in religious fields. Religion is essentially wonderful, but sometimes obstructions by these evil beings create confusion.

The point is that these spirits are filled with frustration, and they are trying to achieve self-realization in one way or another. However, their self-realization takes the form of destruction, of trying to ruin others. Taking pleasure in watching other people suffer as you ruin them is the worst possible mental attitude for a human being. Malign beings thrive at this level.

People's state of mind can vary from high to low. People with the lowest state of mind take pleasure in the misfortune of others, laugh scornfully at them, and wish to cause them even more unhappiness. This is the exact reason religion-related spirits possess people. They possess someone who is overwhelmed by worries and desperate to escape unhappiness. These spirits are getting satisfaction out of ruining a person even further and making them suffer more misery.

However, we cannot blame these spirits completely because there is a part in all of us that feels satisfied when we see another person suffer misfortune. For example, humans feel a sense of relief when they watch someone kill another person in Western movies or period dramas.

It is important, therefore, to establish a strong self that will not be affected by spiritual influences. Worries and wavering create unguarded areas in the mind, which allows religion-related spirits to possess you. When lots of people go to weird spiritual counselors to escape their worries and mental wavering, large numbers of these spirits will dwell there.

The world of spirits is a world of thought, where those with similar thoughts attract each other, and those with different thoughts repel each other. Bodhisattvas of Light and devils repel each other. In the eyes of devils, Bodhisattvas of Light appear evil, whereas to bodhisattvas, devils appear evil.

However, the truth is that good is always on Buddha's side, and this will be evident from the idea of happiness a person holds. Evil spirits are generally self-centered, and they pursue happiness at the cost of others. On the other hand, Buddha smiles upon those who explore happiness from the perspective of improving the world so that everyone can live happily. It is important to understand the difference between these two attitudes.

# 3

## The Spirits of Lust

I would now like to talk about the spirits of lust. In the first section of this chapter, I explained that evil spirits are those who have misused the freedom of mind they were endowed with; the same is true of spirits of lust. Human beings are free to think whatever they want, and since Buddha divided people into males and females, it is only natural that men should be attracted to women and women should be attracted to men. However, this feeling could lead to either good or evil, depending on how it is controlled.

The relationship between men and women is protected by the system of marriage. There is exclusivity in terms of the sexual relationship between a man and a woman. This is because Buddha hopes that men and women will join together to create a home where they can work to build a utopia and that they will achieve happiness this way.

However, if men and women act solely on their physical instincts, there will be huge repercussions. Essentially, men and women have a mission to create a utopia within the home. But sometimes people become blinded by their desire for the opposite sex, such as being attracted physically or to their appearance, and act on that desire. This is not right because it goes against the idea that creating a utopia in the home is the core of creating an ideal society.

Although it is difficult to generalize because there may be complex situations, the important point is whether an individual intends to develop a sexual relationship based on their love for the other person or do so without love. This difference is what separates humankind from animals. What makes human beings human is that they have an inner awareness to discipline themselves in this regard.

Buddha endowed human beings with a sense of shame or feelings of embarrassment; I would like you to stop and consider why this is necessary. Women have an extremely strong sense of shame, but this is a brake mechanism given by Buddha to protect women from becoming corrupted. This sense of shame is also possessed by men. Young people, in particular, tend to have a strong sense of shame; they will restrain themselves from committing wrong deeds when they think they will feel ashamed if they are found out.

A sense of shame is one of the most basic emotions; it protects human beings from degradation. The fact that this feeling exists as a part of our soul shows that we are expected to respect a certain degree of order. The reason we are not free to explore our sexuality at will is that we have been endowed with feelings of shame and embarrassment as an attribute of our soul. Buddha expects us to feel these things. That is the primary reason.

Then why does sexual intercourse between men and women exist? It is because humans have an extremely delicate side to them. If people had to live in a heartless, desert-like world every day, they would become exhausted. For this reason, Buddha granted humans sexual intercourse as a form of joy and pleasure. Humans are allowed this as an act of Buddha's mercy.

If people become obsessed with sexual intercourse, however, they will lose sight of their lofty ideals and the aspiration to better themselves, and this will gradually lead to degradation. From ancient times, there have been numerous taboos connected with sexual matters because young people tend to become obsessed with sex easily. As long as we are born as human beings in this world, we cannot deny our interest in the opposite sex. But at the same time, we must not forget that our souls contain the mechanism to control and adjust this desire. People who exercise their freedom in a way that goes against the true nature of the soul will experience negative consequences and will suffer in hell as spirits of lust.

These spirits of lust attempt to satisfy their cravings by taking possession of people living in this world and leading them astray. This is common in red-light districts. Let's say people go drinking there after work with their colleagues. They will gradually lose their rationality and act on their senses, even though they normally live rationally without being influenced by the spirits of lust. They will begin to crave neon lights, and as they walk through the red-light district, they will often be tempted by spirits of lust and be reduced to becoming just like them.

The bottom line is that people who fall prey to temptations of the flesh have a distorted sense of reason. If they have sound rationality, they will not get involved in this kind of trouble. This is a very important point. So, when dealing with problems related to lust, building a strong sense of reason is an effective solution.

# 4

# Animal Spirits

Some people may have come across the idea of animal spirits, such as snake spirits, spirits of raccoon dogs, and fox spirits. Animals, too, are creatures of Buddha; spirits dwell within their bodies and aim to achieve their own spiritual growth. Therefore, it is only natural that animal spirits exist. You may ask whether animals can also become lost in hell after death. The answer is yes because they, too, experience the emotions of joy, anger, sorrow, and pleasure that are similar to those of human beings.

People may argue that animals do not have minds or are incapable of thinking, but it is a fact that animals are able to think to some extent, and most are capable of experiencing basic emotions. Even small insects have some amount of basic emotions. They want to enjoy pleasure and avoid pain, and they know both joy and sadness. If this is true of insects, then obviously, the more evolved animals are capable of a wider range of emotions. During their repeated reincarnations, animals such as cows, horses, pigs, dogs, and cats have lived in close proximity to human beings, and because of this, they are able to understand what people think to some extent. Some of them are able to think in ways that closely resemble the thinking of humans. However, because animal spirits inhabit animal bodies and are trapped inside an animal form, they are unable to express their emotions adequately in the same way that some humans cannot speak.

So animal spirits really do exist, but the question is, do the spirits of foxes, raccoon dogs, and snakes try to possess and delude humans, as we have been told in tales from the East since ancient times? I would be lying if I were to deny it. These animals are spiritually very strong, and they possess spiritual power. Because they have existed for a long time on earth, undergoing numerous reincarnations, these animals have accumulated various kinds of spiritual power.

Particularly in Japan, there are many negative incidents caused by animal spirits because Japanese people worship animal spirits in various ways. For example, some lost fox spirits inhabit small Shinto shrines through their connection with *Inari* (fox deity) worship. Lots of people worship nature spirits, such as the Shinto gods of water. That is why there are also many snake worshipers, and the same could be said in relation to raccoon dogs.

The souls of these animals are not all plain and without character; they have different tendencies engraved in their souls. Take snakes, for example. Snakes prefer damp places, slither over the ground, and are generally despised by humans. The reason they are so despised may be that they look grotesque and that they also have a vicious, merciless, and vengeful nature. Snake spirits actually have these tendencies in their souls. As a result of exercising the freedom of their souls, they have acquired such tendencies and manifest on earth in the form of snakes.

What about foxes? The foxes in Japanese folktales often deceive people, but do foxes actually have this tendency? Even in the West, foxes are often portrayed as very cunning, but is that really so? In Japan, we enshrine *Inari Daimyojin* (a Shinto god of agriculture and industry), but what is his true identity?

In the Spirit World, Inari Daimyojin is a high spirit living among the various gods in the upper level of the sixth dimension, who guides and trains animal souls. Animal souls are also learning all kinds of things, so they need a teacher. Some animal souls that are more spiritually advanced teach other less advanced animal souls, but there are also human souls that specialize in guiding them. Some human souls control a breed of animals, guide them, and think about how their group as a whole can advance further.

In this way, there are spirits whose role is to guide animals in the Spirit World, and they are trying to help animal souls advance spiritually. Therefore, Inari Daimyojin is one of the position titles in the upper part of the sixth dimensional Light Realm. Numerous spirits take on this role, not just one. Also, most advanced fox spirits work as helpers of Inari Daimyojin. They keep their appearance as foxes and guide the lost fox spirits.

But, unfortunately, when I use my spiritual sight and look at Inari shrines across Japan and the enshrined Inari Daimyojin, I often find a huge mistake. That is, the shrines aren't worshiping gods who are in charge of protecting animals. Instead, they are using the Inari faith to satisfy earthly desires, so people pray for things like their family's safety, passing entrance exams, and success in business. But this is where they are seriously mistaken. The role of Inari Daimyojin is to guide animals, not to help people with things like passing entrance exams, helping them get married, or protecting their health.

Not only that, if people are praying for such things out of earthly desires, those thoughts will accumulate around the shrines and temples. Then, the lost spirits of dead animals become attracted to those desires and gather there. Unlike humans, animals cannot understand anything difficult, but they do possess basic desires such as hunger, the desire to be strong, and the desire to live a long life. So, they are attracted to those desires. They are trying to alleviate their pain by feeding off human desires.

It is said that foxes crave deep-fried tofu. In this way, many lost animal spirits suffer from great hunger. That is why they try to satisfy their hunger by receiving food offerings. However, since they cannot actually eat the food, their desires are unattainable, and eventually, they become uncontrollable desires. They then cause all kinds of harm to humans. For example, they will possess people who give them offerings and cause them to suffer from rheumatism, aching shoulders, or headaches.

On top of that, there are other animal spirits that were not originally animal spirits. There is a part of hell that is known as the Hell of Beasts, which is a realm of animals. Because the other world is a world of thoughts, the inhabitants take on a form that is an exact reflection of their thoughts. For instance, someone who is extremely brutal and vengeful will gradually take on the form of a snake because their thoughts manifest in their external appearance. Someone who enjoys cheating others, thinking only of his own profit and acting in a very egotistical way, will gradually transform into a fox.

As these spirits take on an animal form over several hundreds of years, they begin to believe they really are snakes or foxes. Then they nest in Inari and other shrines and possess and delude people by saying things like, "I am Inari Daimyojin." So there are spirits who believe themselves to be animal spirits when they are, in fact, human souls. They want to be worshiped and given offerings, so they come out pretending to be Inari Daimyojin. This is another kind of animal spirit.

If a spirit has taken the form of an animal for too long, its mind will become tainted with an animalistic consciousness. So, when these spirits no longer feel suffering, which is a characteristic of spirits in hell, and instead feel comfort, they could be regressing as human souls. Therefore, human souls can be born as animals for a period of time, though the number is very small. That is why some dogs express human emotions and why some animals are very fond of humans.

These things sometimes occur as regression in the process of soul evolution, but in the long run, those souls are also developing. By experiencing what it is like to live with animal attributes, they can see the nobility of humans from a different perspective. This experience is similar to that of retired managers or presidents of companies. They had titles while they worked, but once they retired, they became an ordinary person. That is when they truly realize that what they thought was their own power was actually not. Government officials have the same experience; those who used to swagger and thought they were something special when they worked for a government ministry will discover after retirement that they were not as special as their position led them to believe.

What is the fundamental difference between real animal spirits and those human spirits who take on animal form? What it comes down to is that the latter were people who lost their human dignity, who did not attempt to use their freedom for a higher purpose to create something of worth, and who did not take the opportunity they were given. In other words, they are developing spirits who are on the way to mastering a higher degree of freedom to gain back their human dignity.

# 5

## Vengeful Spirits

I would like to finish this chapter by talking about vengeful spirits. They are spirits filled with bitterness and spite. It is often said that the way people meet their death is very important; this is most certainly true. Some people believe that those who die with hatred in their hearts will appear in this world as ghosts. When people die holding strong grudges, they are unable to let go of them even after death. As a result, they possess others or bring others misfortune.

This is not only true of the spirits of the dead but also of *ikiryo* (living ghosts). If a person holds strong feelings of hatred and resentment toward someone, their feelings will be transmitted to the target of their hatred and resentment, day and night. As a result of the vibration of these negative thoughts, the victim will begin to suffer a lot of pain and sometimes become worn out or fall ill. So, if you constantly feel unwell for no particular reason, or if many misfortunes occur in your life, you need to consider whether someone, either dead or alive, has a grudge against you.

If you know of someone who died nursing a grudge against you, try to practice the following: First, study the Truth every day and live according to Happy Science teachings. Secondly, if you did something wrong to the person to make them hate you, sincerely repent for your actions. Thirdly, try to share with them your own enlightenment. You need to help the person realize how wrong and sinful it is to hold onto their hatred and remain lost in the other world. You can achieve this by holding this thought in your mind. If you have truly understood what you have learned, it will be transmitted to the deceased person.

The so-called ikiryo, or the resentment of the living, is also very powerful, sometimes more powerful than the spirits of the dead. Someone may hold grudges, thinking, "He stood in the way of my promotion," "I failed because she tricked me," "My marriage failed because he betrayed me," or "She stole the only person I ever wanted to marry." If you are the target of a lot of this kind of hatred, it is unlikely that you will be able to achieve success or happiness.

One way to free yourself from hatred and resentment of others is by self-reflection. If you believe yourself to be the target of a grudge, you should reflect on why you have incurred this ill will and repent what you think you have done wrong. If you are being targeted as a result of your desires or egotism, you should apologize directly to the person in question, or if this is not possible, ask for forgiveness from that person in your heart.

In some cases, it may all be the result of a misunderstanding. If that is the case, try to explain the true situation. If you cannot do this, reconcile with that person in your heart or ask your guardian and guiding spirits to communicate with the other person's guardian spirit so that the relationship will be mended.

If you reflect on your past and realize that you are at fault, you should do whatever is necessary to solve the problem. Even if you are not responsible for the trouble, do not blame the other person. Instead, if there is something about them that is praiseworthy, then by all means, offer words of praise and try to see the person in a more positive way.

If you have attracted their resentment, it is because you have only been looking at their negative traits. You must stop this. Instead, if you find one thing you dislike about them, discover one good point about them at the same time. If you find three things you do not like about them, think of at least three things you can appreciate about them. You should adopt this way of thinking.

It is true that the mind of someone standing in your way is a mirror that reflects your own thoughts. If your mind changes, you will find that he or she will change too. The reason for attracting the resentment of another person is that both the target and the holder of the resentment either do not see the other person in high regard or have ignored the other person. If, after considering these two possibilities, you feel that you shoulder some of the responsibility, you should apologize honestly or look for the other person's good points to praise or appreciate. This is the way to free yourself from the resentment or grudges of either those who have already passed away or those still living.

No one enjoys being hated by another, and those who are hated by others cannot get ahead in life, so try not to attract the resentment of others. To achieve this, you should live every day in a humble way with gratitude.

If you attract someone's hatred without hurting them, it is either because you try to gather the love of others all for yourself or because you have a tendency to show off. It is because you are ostentatious about something or you appear too proud to others. So, if you tend to be the object of other people's resentment, it is because you still aren't humble enough; you are lacking humility, a sense of gratitude, and an egoless heart. You need to think about how to live with a selfless heart.

I have described the various types of evil spirits. Each of them could easily be found in a person's inner world. If you find any of these symptoms in your own mind, stop your mind and start practicing self-reflection. When you find something wrong in your thoughts, apologize sincerely to Buddha and vow not to make the same mistake again. In this way, those who always correct their mistakes and aim for further spiritual growth with a pure heart are the ones who are truly living in accordance with Buddha's Truth.

# CHAPTER FIVE

# Confronting Evil Spirits

# 1

# Expand Your Knowledge of Spiritual Matters

In this chapter, I would like to talk about how to confront evil spirits and overcome their delusions and spiritual possessions.

The first thing we must be aware of is that people do not have an accurate understanding of spiritual matters; they are unaware of the true nature of evil spirits, so they do not know how to handle them. When you are physically ill, a doctor can prescribe you medicine or perform an operation to treat you. However, when it comes to emotional and mental suffering, almost no one can provide a prescription for you. Each person is acting as their own physician and writing their own prescription in their own way. This gives rise to various mistakes.

Professional religious practitioners should essentially be "doctors of the soul" who prescribe cures for maladies of the soul. Today, however, there are so many "immoral doctors," and it has become difficult for us to receive satisfactory treatment for the soul. For this reason, we need to pay due respect to true spiritual knowledge, and doing so will promote the advancement in psychiatry or medical studies of the mind.

In medical science, there is a comprehensive system of theories to back up clinical treatment, and doctors can cure patients with different illnesses because they have this medical knowledge. As for spirituality, on the other hand, there is a lack of basic theories, and this is where the problem lies. Today, different religions are competing with one another as each religion claims to be the only true religion. The main concern for the general public is which religions to believe. Unlike in medical science, there is no one who studies religion to see which is the most effective one overall.

Medical science is roughly divided into Western and Eastern medicine, and doctors in each field are objectively exploring the effects of its cures and remedies. Nevertheless, in the field of spirituality, there is no clear knowledge about the effects of its cures or treatments. So, the problem is that although there are subjective assessments of its cures, there are no objective standards when it comes to spiritual matters.

When confronting evil spirits, you must have abundant spiritual knowledge. First, you must know the true nature of these spirits. Evil spirits are not foreign beings that are unrelated to you. They are simply souls suffering from an illness of the mind, and you, too, could become one of them. So, if you return to the other world with this illness of the mind, you will most likely become an evil spirit.

What does it mean to suffer from an illness of the mind? It means that, at the very least, you are not filled with happiness. You are worrying about something, oftentimes about negative things. At times, people may feel very negative about themselves or become obsessed with negative feelings toward other people. If people find themselves in these extreme states, they will begin to suffer, for example, from a desire that knows no contentment, complaints, dissatisfaction, skepticism, frustration, inferiority complex, and self-assertion. Their behavior is similar to a fly trapped inside a small glass box, flying round and round, battering itself against the walls without realizing it is confined. This is the way human beings behave when they are caught in a vortex of worry.

For this reason, it is important that you consider whether you have any possibility of becoming an evil spirit. Some may say that they are unhappy because they are under some kind of negative spiritual disturbance or that their ancestors became lost. But you have to know that you yourself could also become a lost spirit after you die.

The principle, "like attracts like," is one of the laws that underlies this world and the next. There is a good reason for evil spirits to be drawn to particular people; these people have certain elements within them that attract these spirits. By looking at the kind of evil spirit you are possessed by and suffering from, you will understand what kind of mistaken thoughts you have in your mind. In this sense, we can say that an evil spirit is like a tutor. People who are possessed by evil spirits are not leading calm, peaceful, and happy lives. It also indicates that a person still has a long way to go on the path to enlightenment.

To enter the path to enlightenment, you should not rely on outside power to expel evil spirits. Instead, it is essential that you look within yourself, expel the evil spirits from your mind, and remove the negative energy that may turn you into an evil spirit. There is an expression, "the devil within." It tells us that everyone has seeds of evil in their minds that can invite evil from the outside.

After all, confronting evil spirits does not mean fighting with the evil spirits that are outside of you; it is a confrontation with your own mind. Evil spirits cannot inhabit people who are bright, cheerful, unattached, and filled with light in their hearts. Evil spirits cannot get close to such people. Therefore, you must quickly think about how you can restore a mind that is as clear as the blue sky. If you do not do this and instead stay gloomy and indecisive, your mind will never be clear. A mind that invites evil spirits can be likened to a sky covered with rain clouds. Even though the sun is always shining behind the clouds, it will not shine through unless the clouds are cleared away. Likewise, the clouds in your mind will block out Buddha's light.

So, the first thing you need to do is to clear away these clouds. To do this, you should carefully examine what kind of rain clouds are over your mind. Then, you will know what you need to do to clear them away. Worries are what you constantly think about or thoughts that your mind always reverts to. Human beings cannot worry about two things at once. You may seem to have a number of worries, but in most cases, they all stem from a single cause. This single cause is the key or the core of all your worries and the one that can cause the most damage to your life. So, it is necessary to tackle the core of the problem head-on.

What makes you suffer may be a single thought or something imagined. "That person is making me miserable" is one thought, and it can be the cause of your suffering. Also, the things that other people say to you can make you suffer. While one person thinks nothing of a particular comment, the same words may cause another person five or ten years of pain. What is the difference between these two people? I would like to explore this further in the next section.

# 2

# Self-Conviction

People will react in different ways to the same external circumstances. For example, if someone speaks ill of another, its effect will vary depending on the person on the receiving end. Some people will simply ignore a hurtful remark and forget it altogether, whereas others will feel as if an unremovable arrow has penetrated deep into their hearts, causing them endless pain. In other cases, some people accept criticisms and reflect on themselves with humility, then try to correct their wrongdoings but ignore off-the-mark comments. In this way, there are many different types of people, but one thing I can say is that the key to life lies in how you accept or let go of external events or phenomena that fall upon you.

I would like to emphasize here that one of the most important things for you is self-conviction. Self-conviction does not mean overestimating your abilities or being conceited; it is the indescribable confidence that comes from the realization that you are not such a bad person after all.

When people are in the midst of pain or sorrow, they tend to become negative about themselves and think endlessly about how bad or sinful a person they are. However, it is important to see yourself with a more objective eye and tell yourself that you are not as bad a person as you might think.

When you look back on your entire life, you might say, "I was wrong about this point" or "I should have done better there." But at the same time, you will recognize that you did not live such a bad life. It means you will realize that you have been loved by Buddha. You will be convinced that you have been of service to others.

Self-confidence comes from the accumulation of small convictions. You should look at yourself on various occasions every day and, little by little, discover the self who has been of service to others. Without doing these things, you cannot have true self-conviction.

Waterfowl floating on the surface of a pond have a coating of oil on their feathers that repels water. Self-conviction works in the same way. No matter what misfortunes occur, self-conviction acts like this oil so that they do not harm the depths of your heart.

For example, the amount of emotional damage caused by the death of a parent, a sibling, or someone close to you varies from person to person. Some people grieve over these things for up to 10 years, others suddenly grow gray hair and fall ill, yet others are able to carry on serenely with their lives. When a loved one passes away, it is important to be grateful for everything that person did for you while they were alive and tell yourself that from now on, you will stand on your own two feet.

Whatever the case, the important mindset is to believe in Buddha. "Since Buddha created this world, what may appear sad must have some purpose or meaning. There is no way Buddha intends to simply cause me pain." "Maybe I can become stronger through experiencing the death of my family member." "Maybe I parted ways with my friend to meet someone even more wonderful." "I broke up with my partner, but maybe I will find an even better match." Please think in this way. As you endure this time, you should create a store of inner strength while you treasure yourself. Instead of struggling in pain and drowning in misery, you should work on refining your soul.

At times like this, what is vital is to hold on to your faith in Buddha and your love for Him. When you are caught up in a vortex of worry, ask yourself if you haven't forgotten your love for Buddha. Most people become obsessed with love for themselves. All they can think about is how pitiful they are. They are desperate for the sympathy of others, but others do not sympathize with them. The problem lies in this very thought.

At such times, straighten your back and look up at the open sky. People who are in the midst of worry and at the mercy of evil spirits, in general, crouch down, turn their backs on the sun, and gaze only at their own small shadow. As long as they do this, they will never be able to see the light.

So stand up straight and stretch out toward the sun. This shows that you have the love for Buddha. Do not be entrapped by the small image you hold of yourself, but instead, turn toward Buddha and be thankful. You need to realize how vast the love you have been given is. You must try and think that although you may be unhappy now, what is happening is not so serious from a long-term point of view. In fact, you should think that such experience provides you with nourishment for further progress.

No matter what trials await you, as long as you remember that you are learning lessons from each problem, you will only become greater. If you have an indomitable spirit, things that seem difficult will never defeat you; rather, they will strengthen you. People who are free and independent and who have an indomitable spirit will never be completely defeated by hardships. To sum up, whatever the adversities you face, it is essential to see them as a hammer to temper and forge you.

# 3

# Self-Reflection

Next, I would like to talk about self-reflection. We cannot talk about confronting evil spirits without considering self-reflection. Self-reflection may seem a rather passive approach, but it is, in fact, an excellent method of confronting evil spirits.

By observing the words and behavior of those who are possessed by evil spirits, you will understand why self-reflection is an excellent method. What these people have in common is that they claim nothing is their fault. They make complaints such as, "The social system was bad," "It was the company's fault," "He harmed me," "I'm unlucky because I don't come from a good family," "It is because I was born in the countryside," "It is my parents' fault that I'm not taller."

In this way, they blame external factors, which is a characteristic of evil spirits. If you find this tendency within yourself, you should think that you are either possessed by evil spirits or are a prime candidate for becoming one in the future. You need to realize that when you try to attribute the cause of your misfortune to outside factors, you are at the mercy of evil spirits.

In this case, it is essential to practice self-reflection. Self-reflection means looking back and examining yourself.

When you feel like blaming others, you must look within yourself. But how should you do this?

First, you should ask yourself whether the cause of the discord lies not only with the other person but also with you. Check and see whether or not any problems originated on your side. Then, if you discover that you have made a mistake, apologize to the person either in person or in your mind. Next, ask Buddha for His forgiveness and resolve never to make the same mistake again.

A baby is born naked and knows nothing of this world, but as he grows up, he accumulates many experiences and learns many lessons through trial and error. It is what he learns through this process that matters most. You should always have a positive attitude toward learning. Self-reflection is one way of learning. Human beings undergo many new experiences in the course of their lives, and if you think you have made a mistake at some point, you need to reflect on what you did.

The traditional Buddhist way of undertaking self-reflection is through the Eightfold Path.

The first component of the Eightfold Path is Right View, which means looking at things in the right way. This is checking to see whether you view others and yourself objectively through the eyes of a third person.

People are apt to see others and themselves from an arbitrary, biased perspective. They think, "He was born into a bad family, that is why he behaves in that way," "He only has one parent, so he must have a warped mind," "He is poor, so he must have an inferiority complex about it," "Rich people are arrogant, and they exploit the poor," or "Famous people are all the same." People tend to make these sorts of sweeping generalizations and simplistic judgments about others. They quickly make assumptions about how people should be, for example, "A religious person should be like this," or "A professional athlete should be like that."

However, the truth is that people are all different, even within the field of their profession. It is almost impossible to understand a person's feelings after only a short acquaintance. Take, for instance, people working in the same office. A working woman has her own worries, and a new employee has his own. A mid-level manager also has worries specific to his or her position. Everyone has worries of one kind or another.

It is difficult to see others correctly; you may not be able to do so even if you spend your whole life trying. You should never forget the possibility that although you see someone in a particular way, there may be a completely different way of seeing them.

The same can be said of yourself. You probably have certain beliefs about what kind of person you are, but you should be open to the possibility that you may appear completely different from another perspective.

Next comes Right Speech. The practice of Right Speech is most important in confronting evil spirits. When evil spirits possess people, the first sign of their influence will show in people's speech. Those who are always speaking ill of others and who are always complaining and grumbling are most likely under negative spiritual influence. If you find yourself speaking negatively, you should think about why you are doing this and make an effort to use more positive language. This effort will set you on a path to a happier life.

The Eightfold Path also includes Right Effort, in other words, making an effort to follow the path to Buddha in the right way. Evil spirits are only concerned with corrupting people and are filled with a desire to make others suffer the same pain as they themselves endure. So, they are very weak against people with aspirations and who make efforts.

However, there are those with aspirations who are still deluded by evil spirits. They are the ones who become arrogant quickly, who are self-assertive, or who are self-centered. On the other hand, evil spirits cannot affect those who are reflecting on themselves with humility and constantly moving forward; there is no way they can influence these people. This is the reality.

Someone qualified in a martial art, such as karate or judo, will usually be polite and well-mannered. Those who are truly strong treat others gently. For example, someone who is 6-Dan in kendo will not want to hit another person's head with a stick, and someone who is 5-Dan in judo will not feel the need to throw a stranger he meets on the street.

On the other hand, gangster-like delinquents will vandalize things and lash out at others. But they have little intention to put that energy constructively into sports or martial arts. In fact, they have no intention of making Right Effort. If these people really want to prove how strong they are, they should do it through martial arts such as judo, kendo, or karate, but they never do. In contrast, those who have trained properly in sports or martial arts are gentle and considerate toward others. Here lies the difference between people who become evil spirits and those who do not. If you make a genuine effort to follow the right path, you will improve yourself, and you will eventually be free from any desire to hurt others.

Right Will is to focus your mind on living in accordance with Buddha's Truth. This is also important in the Eightfold Path. When practicing self-reflection, the aspect of controlling your will should not be neglected; you need to be aware of your will throughout the day. Your will is you, yourself. What differentiates a saint from an ordinary person is the content of their thoughts. The thoughts that occupy a saint's mind all day are different from the thoughts of an ordinary person, and the same is true of the thoughts of high spirits. They view things from a higher perspective, think about things from a broader, richer, and more generous standpoint, and always wish to guide as many people as possible.

On the other hand, ordinary people are interested only in themselves, and they look at things from this perspective; their use of will is very different from that of a saint. The same holds true for how people approach others. There is a huge difference between those who approach others with the intention of guiding them and the intention of hurting them.

In fact, people who should be most admired in this world are those who are always thinking of the happiness of as many people as possible. During the course of your life, you should sincerely wish for the happiness of as many people as possible and then actually take some action. This is how humans really should be. Therefore, I would like you to examine your will at least once a day.

The Eightfold Path also includes the path of Right Thought, which means to think in the right way. The "thought" of Right Thought refers to what comes into and what goes out of your mind. You need to observe the thoughts that enter your mind as you face the many different situations in a day and control these thoughts. In contrast, the "will" of Right Will refers to the intention or direction of what you will do in the future. So, in practicing Right

Will, you are required to make an effort to ensure that your will is not focused in the wrong direction but is continuously directed toward Buddha.

In this way, through practicing self-reflection, you will discover your true self that is well-balanced. It is the *you* that is undistorted, well-shaped, and highly refined. By becoming well-balanced, you will leave no room for evil spirits to delude you. Evil spirits always try to attack a person at his or her weakest point; this is one of their characteristics. They will concentrate their energy on the darkness, dent, or protrusion in a person, so you should try not to create these things within your mind.

In this context, you can say that self-reflection is the best defense against evil spirits. While being the best defense, it is also the most powerful offense because, in the process of defending yourself, you give off thoughts that evil spirits despise. Just as mosquitoes hate to be near mosquito-repelling incense, these spirits do not want to approach someone who practices self-reflection. An evil spirit is like a mosquito; if "mosquitoes" are flying around trying to suck your blood, you should emit things they dislike the most, like the smoke emitting from a mosquito-repelling incense.

In the end, what evil spirits hate most is the right way of living. To restore the right way of living, you need to practice self-reflection. By doing this, you will be able to prevent these spirits from coming near you.

# 4

## The Philosophy of Positive Thinking

The next method of confronting evil spirits is the philosophy of positive thinking. Those who are involved in religious matters will become spiritually sensitive, and they may sometimes be on the receiving end of various spiritual disturbances. They often feel unwell, and their head feels heavy when evil spirits approach them.

One of the most effective measures against this is positive thinking, which is the idea of dispelling darkness with light. It is very difficult to extinguish darkness, but by making an effort to increase the light, the darkness will naturally disappear. If you are in a pitch-black room, it is impossible to disperse the darkness, but once you turn on the light, the darkness will disappear. If it is still dark with one candle, light another, then another. This is positive thinking. If there were numerous muggings on a particular street at night, we would solve this problem by increasing the number of streetlights to make the area better lit. Just as thieves find it hard to come out on brightly lit streets, the same reasoning can be applied in dealing with the darkness in your mind.

To think positively and live cheerfully has the effect of preventing negative situations from happening. This has been proven through many people's experiences in their lives. Who do you feel more inclined toward, someone who is always smiling or someone with a sour expression? Have you ever thought of a smiling person as ugly? No matter who smiles, a smile is beautiful. A smile is something that has been given to us as a form of compassion. Will anyone be displeased to see someone cheerful? Will anyone dislike a person for smiling too much? Those who say such things are likely possessed by evil spirits. Normally, people are happy and refreshed to meet someone with a bright nature.

So, one method of expelling evil spirits is to radiate a stronger light. Instead of trying to remove or fight against evil spirits, you can expel them by increasing your inner light, that is to say, by making your thoughts more positive and radiating the light of your inner self.

Everyone has some darkness in their mind, "the devil within," which invites evil spirits. So first, it is essential to eliminate this darkness with light. The darkness consists mostly of negative emotions, such as worries and complaints. In most cases, worries about the future and complaints about the past attract evil spirits.

But is it really true that your past was filled with unhappiness? Certainly, you may have experienced a lot of suffering, but you somehow managed to get over it. If you think back on your life and see nothing but a succession of failures, you have an unbalanced way of seeing things. It may be true that you have experienced failure, but it is very unlikely that your whole life has been a failure. So the problem does not lie in the facts but rather in the way you judge them; you may have smeared your past with a black crayon.

Positive thinking is one method of transforming a "black" assessment into a golden one. Although you may have experienced many kinds of pain and suffering in the past, it is the lessons you have learned and the value gained from these experiences that become the material to make your life shine brilliantly.

People can learn many things through failure. Thomas Edison is said to have experienced hundreds of failures before finally succeeding in inventing the electric light bulb. However, for Edison, who practiced positive thinking, they were not failures but rather proofs that certain methods did not lead to success. This is how he interpreted his experience.

In the same way, instead of writing off failure simply as failure, you should tell yourself that you have learned which methods should be discarded because they are not viable. Then, the next time you encounter a similar situation, you will simply take a different path.

Your past is neither a curse that binds you nor something that brings you bad luck. Rather, it provides you with the material for self-improvement and presents a range of ways that should be avoided in the future to achieve happiness. Your past will appear marvelous from this perspective.

As for the future, it is essential to have the self-confidence to believe that no matter what happens, you will somehow be able to get over it. Those who have a strong sense of unhappiness and believe that the future is going to punish them are overly concerned with themselves. When you are overly self-concerned, you start believing that by imagining the worst that could ever happen to you, you will not have to prepare for anything worse. But this attitude only leads to unhappiness.

Instead, you should think, "Yesterday, things worked themselves out. Today will manage itself as well. I'm sure tomorrow will work out, too." It is important to think in such a positive way. Even if it is true that the earth will crack and the world will be in turmoil tomorrow, there is nothing positive about worrying about it today. It is all the more important to live today believing that tomorrow will be brilliant.

Another important aspect of positive thinking is the realization of your thoughts. The thoughts of human beings will eventually be realized. If you have positive, constructive thoughts, you will find yourself in positive and constructive situations. But if your mind is filled with passive, negative thoughts, the same sort of passive and negative situations will unfold around you.

In this respect, we can positively evaluate the techniques of self-actualization popular today because a bright future will indeed open before those who are constantly planting positive, constructive thoughts in their minds. I would like all of you to succeed in achieving self-realization in the right way. Discover your future self that shines brilliantly, and use this image to achieve magnificent success.

I believe that the biggest self-realization for a human being is through broadening and deepening one's character, having a positive influence on as many people as possible, and guiding others in the right direction. It is essential to walk this path with courage. As long as you lack positive ideas and are overwhelmed by dark, negative emotions, you will never find happiness. I would like you to value the philosophy of positive thinking as the basis for happiness and to value self-actualization as a method to practice this philosophy.

# 5

## Immersing Yourself in Work

I would like to finish this chapter on confronting evil spirits by talking about immersing yourself in your work. To sum up, those who have problems with negative spiritual influences have openings in their minds that allow evil spirits to sneak in. If people are caught up with worries and suffering and live life in frustration, these spirits will find a way in. So, in order to not leave any areas of your mind unguarded, you should immerse yourself in what is most important to you. In other words, pour the greatest part of your energy into what you think is of the greatest value.

If you are influenced by evil spirits, do not spend too much time thinking about them. Concentrate on what you need to do in the present, namely, the work you have at hand.

Evil spirits are no excuse, just as being hurt by someone's comments is no excuse, either. Just as it is up to the person who speaks to determine what they want to say, it is up to you to determine how you receive what others say to you. You should not blame others or your environment for being hurt. Instead of giving way to pessimistic thoughts or negative emotions, you should concentrate on what you think is most important. If you are wasting time worrying, instead use that time to take a positive step, even if it is only a small one.

Human beings cannot think of two things at once, so when you are preoccupied with worries, immerse yourself in your work. For instance, you could find new ideas each day to improve the way you usually do things and make progress; with this attitude, you will eventually be able to achieve great success. Ask yourself if your work is becoming routine and monotonous. Ask yourself if there are better ways of doing it, if you can create more time for yourself, or if you can spend your time doing something more meaningful. So, if you are in the midst of worry or suffering, put all your energy into your work. By immersing yourself in activity and keeping busy, you will find a way to solve your problems.

For instance, cold-hearted people may criticize you harshly about your work, but getting upset is of no use. You should take it as a stimulus to do better. Tell yourself that being criticized means you still have a long way to go in your work and that you have to accumulate further good results. If you can think in this way, then the more you are criticized, the better the results you will achieve. At that time, those criticisms you received will be something to be thankful for. When others praise you at work, you will feel happy and make more progress in your work. On the other hand, when others are criticizing or bad-mouthing you, if you can perceive that they are saying so because you are not making enough effort, you can be more humble and make more effort.

Buddha will certainly open up a path for those who are always trying to move forward no matter what, and so will the people in this world. They will surely open the path for those people who keep moving forward. Don't you feel touched when seeing a frog trying to jump onto a willow leaf, no matter how many times it fails? That being said, humans are deeply moved by seeing those who are courageously making their way forward with strong convictions, no matter the criticisms they receive and how much they are blamed. You may be obsessed over different kinds of worries and anxieties at times, but those are the times you must become resolute and hold on to your convictions.

I have just explained that immersing yourself in your work and leading a busy life is an effective method of winning against evil spirits. I would like you to always remember this. If you are overwhelmed by worries, try to increase the amount of time you are working or take on a new task. If you are a housewife, try not to restrict yourself to your usual routine but instead study something new and use your time in creative ways.

To conclude, by turning your mind in more productive and constructive directions, you can confront and overcome evil spirits and develop yourself into an even more wonderful person. Soon, the time will come when you realize that those who appeared to be evil spirits actually served as your teachers to help you refine your soul. It is my heartfelt wish that everyone develops a positive, constructive, and cheerful outlook on life.

# CHAPTER SIX

# An Unshakable Mind

# 1

## The Awareness That
## You Are a Child of Buddha

In this last chapter, I would like to talk about an unshakable mind, which is the very title of this book. The Japanese word for an unshakable mind is *fudo-shin*, which means "a mind that does not move." From long ago, an unshakable mind has been considered extremely important in Buddhism because most suffering and delusion in life stem from the wavering of the mind. One of the main themes for Buddhist seekers has been to find ways to establish a mind that does not waver.

This does not only apply to Buddhist seekers. If you look at the people around you and the people you meet at various points in your life, you may notice that those with an unshakable mind have deep inner peace and are strong and reliable at the same time. Their determination to overcome any difficulty and their strong convictions are what build their foundation to become a leader. What makes a leader a leader is their mind that never sways by minor difficulties. They have the strength to tackle problems with a big heart, and what lies beneath this strength is an unshakable mind. Many people claim they have self-confidence but lose it the moment a difficulty occurs, such as getting blamed for small mistakes. What these people need is to grasp a truly unshakable mind.

To achieve this, it is vital that you awaken to the fact that you are a child of Buddha. Without this understanding, an unshakable mind is superficial. Our minds will not waver when we recognize that we are connected to Buddha in the very depths of our hearts. Without this awareness, we will wander aimlessly in our lives, like leaves floating on waves. If you are convinced that you are a child of Buddha, as if you are a boat anchored on the seabed, you will be stable. The weight of the anchor hooked into the seabed keeps the boat stable and prevents it from drifting. In life, what serves as an anchor is your awareness as a child of Buddha and the belief that you are connected to Him. If you hold to this single truth, you will manage to get through the adversities in life.

However, if your belief in this wavers and you accept the idea that you are at the mercy of destiny, like a leaf floating on the river of fate, then nothing can help you. This will only make you hold pessimistic thoughts, such as thinking that others and the environment will harm you or that a tragic future awaits you. Whether you choose to live an unhappy life influenced by these sorts of fatalistic ideas or a positive life full of confidence depends on who you believe yourself to be. Those who have realized that they are children of Buddha and have awakened to their true nature as children of Buddha are incredibly strong.

People who have managed to find confidence in themselves in the midst of severe ordeals are also strong. The following are often also said: to know one's absolute limits is important; those who know how far they can push themselves physically or capability-wise are strong; and oftentimes, people who have experienced war and lived on the edge of life and death have nerves of steel.

From ancient times, it has been said that for people to become a great person, they need to have experienced some kind of difficulty or suffering, such as a serious illness, failing a university entrance exam, heartbreak, a divorce, or job loss. These kinds of hardships are considered a prerequisite for greatness because suffering and difficulty allow us to confirm where the rock bottom of life is or the lowest you can fall. Those who have confirmed the "ground" that lies at the depth of their heart can become stronger. They can fight off any difficulties and get back on their feet again. Every time you face a difficulty, you should learn your limit as to how much you can endure. If you can see the situations in this way, it becomes easier to find positive significance in distress or difficulty; you will come to know how far you can exert your strength when you are really driven into a corner.

It is often said that, to assess someone's ability, you only need to see the person when they are at the top of triumph and in the depths of despair. Those who expose their egos and become conceited at the moment of victory are mediocre people, and so are those who wail or cry out in times of despair. But those who can carry on with life as usual with an unshakable mind in both extreme situations are extraordinary for this reason alone.

Take Thomas Edison as an example, the great inventor who, after many experiments, obtained patents for a number of different inventions. He once watched his laboratory burn down in a fire. When he knew that it had been reduced to ashes, he simply said, "Good, now I can make a fresh start."

A similar incident happened to the British historian and essayist, Thomas Carlyle. One day, Carlyle asked a friend to read a manuscript he had been working on. After the friend finished reading it, he left it on his desk and fell asleep. When he got up, he found that his maid thought it was waste paper and discarded it. When Carlyle heard what had happened, instead of being filled with regret or anxiety, he simply started to write the entire book again from the beginning. After its completion, the manuscript went on to become a famous history book and was described as an immortal masterpiece. I see great strength in his attitude. No matter what difficulties you may encounter, have a firm will and the strength to start from scratch again. Even if your work was to be destroyed right before its completion, have the perseverance to start all over again. This kind of attitude is very important.

People who believe they can start afresh from nothing at any time are strong. In contrast, people who become afraid of losing their position and try to cling to it when they attain a certain level of status or fame are weak, unstable, and fragile. Let us be like Edison, who said it was a chance to make a fresh start when his laboratory burned to the ground. Let us have the persistence of Carlyle, who lost his manuscript but rewrote it, which later became an immortal piece of literature. I am moved more by the mindset of these great figures than by their actual achievements.

Dale Carnegie, who is famous for his books *How to Win Friends and Influence People* and *How to Stop Worrying and Start Living*, had a similar trait. When he was young, he wanted to be a novelist, but the manuscripts of the two novels he wrote were both rejected by publishers. After this, he did not attempt to write any more novels. He instead wrote many wonderful books about positive thinking and self-improvement, and they inspired many people throughout the world. Carnegie never regretted that he could not become a novelist. He was glad to have chosen another path. When he was told that he would never become a novelist, he was shocked and felt as if he had come to the end of the road. However, he successfully got over it and went on to become a thinker and educator. In this way, he succeeded in carving out a new path for himself.

Good fortune can be found everywhere. If you are always willing to open up a bright future wherever you are, there will be no suffering or difficulty. The deeper you awaken to the truth that you are a child of Buddha, the more you should value the indomitable spirit that says no matter what happens, you will get back on your feet.

# 2

# Diamond in the Rough

I have explained the importance of being aware that you are a child of Buddha. This can also be explained in another way, using the example of a diamond in the rough. There is a world of difference between people who see themselves as worthless pebbles and those who see themselves as unpolished diamonds. When you believe that your true self is a diamond, the more you polish your own self, the more brilliantly you will shine, and the light you radiate will encourage you.

However, people are prone to sink into self-pity and think they are useless or worthless. Some people even live their lives in ways that help them confirm their identity as losers. Each time they experience a misfortune such as heartbreak, failure in a job, or illness, they think they are good for nothing and spend their lives reaffirming this to themselves.

But this attitude is not right. These people have lost sight of the uncut diamond within. No matter how hopeless a person may appear to be, he or she is not inferior to others; it only means that they have not refined their inner self as much as others. You should always bear this in mind.

The more you refine yourself, the more brilliantly you will shine. People will see you either as a pebble or a jewel, depending on the strength of your brilliance. It is only a matter of course that those who think they are useless will be regarded in the same way by others. How you face your weakness and overcome it is the important point. Unless you overcome your sense of inferiority, you will never be able to make a true leap in life.

Then, how can people who have the tendency to blame themselves discover the truth that they are not pebbles but unpolished diamonds? People who have a habit of self-blaming can be divided into two types. One type is those who perceive everything about themselves negatively when they fail at something. They tend to have such negative mindsets. The other type is those who are usually very confident, but when something crushes their confidence, they completely lose the sense of their own worth.

However, you should not see yourself in a completely negative way nor adopt an all-or-nothing attitude. Do not forget that, while you do have negative traits, you also have good points. Without a doubt, there is good within you. Even if one person may talk about you in a negative way, there will always be someone else who will praise you. Only very few people in this world will live their lives without being praised. Even a social outcast who lives in the shadows must have some good points; you can always find something to praise about them. If this is so, why is it so difficult to find the good points in yourself, who is the most precious to you? Look carefully at yourself through the eyes of an impartial third party and see if you can perceive your own wonderful, radiant nature.

When you suffer from a setback, you may feel as though you have lost everything, but that is actually not true. Rather, setbacks may be showing you your wonderful side or stripping away your false self that was formed from you leading a false life worrying too much about how others see you. If you can think this way, you still have hope. Even if you experience failure in this world, it does not negate your entire self-worth. Your good points are still there. Unless you adopt this sort of impartial view, you will never be able to discover the uncut diamond within you.

In contrast, some people go too far in the opposite direction and become overconfident. They think that they are simply marvelous and develop an unapproachable personality. They believe that they are truly wonderful and the best in the world, so they do not take advice from others, and they think that anyone who does not hold them in high regard is mistaken. This certainly leads to problems. This sort of person cannot live in heaven. Heaven is a place where harmonious people go to. So, people who keep others away or who consider someone they cannot get along with as their enemy can never live there.

Rather than these attitudes, you should try and find a way in which you and others can coexist. If you have no intention of changing or improving yourself, you cannot say you are refining the unpolished diamond within. No one would wear a dirty diamond ring in public and say, "A diamond is a diamond whether or not it is covered in mud." I am sure you would clean and polish the diamond beforehand. In the same way, it is important that you carefully polish your mind, which is a diamond in the rough. People often comment on what others wear, making remarks like, "How can she come to the party wearing such clothes," but how come people are so indifferent when it comes to the "clothing" of their mind? Can you show up in front of someone who has a high level of enlightenment with stains on the garments of your mind? An enlightened person would instantly identify the stains.

What I am trying to say here is that you also need to "attire" your mind. Even if you own a beautiful garment made from British material, it will become dirty if you do not send it to the dry cleaners. You send your clothes to the dry cleaners and have them washed, so why won't you do the same with your mind instead of leaving it stained and unwashed? Please think about this. You must make your mind beautiful, too.

It is because you wash your dishes every day that you can enjoy delicious meals. If you placed food on unwashed plates, it would not taste very good. You can always buy or replace the dishes, but you still wash the dishes every day. So why do you leave your minds unwashed? We wash something simple such as our dishes every day, so let's start washing our minds every day, too. If you think this is too much trouble, there is something wrong. How can you meet others and proudly state your opinions with such a mind you ought to be ashamed of? You need to continue to reflect on these points.

# 3

# Breaking Through Delusions

In this section, I would like to discuss how to break through delusions. To begin with, let us consider what a delusion is. When you are deluded, your heart and mind are torn apart by conflicting emotions. When you feel trapped in a situation where things have become so entangled that you cannot see the path to the solution, you could say you are in the grip of delusion.

At such times, you need to discover how to cut your way through the difficulties and find a way out. To find a way out, it is important that you check and see you are not denying your own potential or you are not limiting yourself. Sometimes, your presumptions may be mistaken.

For example, people have worries about work. Those who have specialized in their job for a long time may fear not being able to make a living doing any other work. But they need to ask themselves why they believe this. If this is the case for you, is it really true that you cannot do any other job besides the one you specialize in? I would like you to ask yourself why you lack the courage and confidence to leave your job and why you cannot believe you will earn a living doing some other kind of work.

Some men attribute their reasons for not having the job they would like to their wives or children and say, "Year after year, I have been doing a job that doesn't really suit me for your sake, and I will continue to do it until the day I retire. If it had not been for you, I would have been free to choose any job I wanted, but because of you, I could not." In saying this, these men try to impose a sense of guilt on their wives and children. In reality, it is their own problem. But because they do not have enough confidence in themselves, they cannot help but complain in this way.

People also worry about their health. Many people are anxious that one day, they will become ill or get into an accident. These worries are quite prevalent today. Medical and health insurance have currently become part of our lives. These systems are effective from the standpoint of social welfare. However, if they are based on the idea that human beings naturally fall ill, that is a grave mistake.

Human beings can essentially live out their life without getting ill so much. You need to realize that illness is often created by the very idea that illness exists. People tend to think, "If I get sick, I can go to the doctor" or "If I take medicine, I will be safe." This sort of thinking may be acceptable for people in poor health, but it might be necessary to stop taking medicine for once.

Human beings are healthy by nature, and their bodies are not made to get sick so easily. If you have a strong belief in health, your body will naturally become stronger. For example, if you trust your digestive organs, they will work well, but if you do not trust them and always take digestive medicine, they will gradually become weaker.

When you get anxious about your health, you need to find the child of Buddha within you. The human body is not supposed to get ill so easily. In a situation where there are no doctors or medicine, most illnesses would heal naturally. Doctors know very well that it is essentially the power of the patient that cures their illness. Medication and medical treatment can only aid the process of healing. If the human body did not have the power to heal, surgical incisions would never heal. Wounds close thanks to the body's natural power of healing.

Other common worries are about money or one's financial situation. People are often afraid that they will not earn enough in the future or that their income will not increase anymore. One of the reasons this fear arises is a lack of confidence in their own abilities. But in this world, there are many jobs where you can create wealth. The sort of job that produces wealth is one that caters to a great demand. The types of work that produce wealth are the ones that meet people's demands, whereas jobs that do not meet any demand do not produce any wealth.

People always have needs in every era; they are always searching for something. It is important to be sensitive and to know what this "something" is. If you succeed in supplying what people want, it will bring wealth both to you and others.

For example, if you publish a book that people wish to read, it will certainly become a best-seller. Not only will it enrich the minds of many, but it will also make the writer wealthy. This principle applies to work, too. Work that you develop by considering the needs of people today will thrive. The same goes for songs. Songs that people want to hear will become a hit, but no matter how many new songs you release, if people do not like them, they will not be listened to.

What is important is to develop an ability or a sensor to discover the needs of people. If you are capable of this, the path to success will open before you. So, if you are worried financially, always think about what people want at the present time and what you can do to benefit others. By considering these points, you may easily solve your financial worries.

So far, I have described worries about employment, illness, and money that people in this age seem to suffer from. Apart from these, there are also worries that arise from human relationships. This is inevitable. People create suffering in all kinds of relationships, such as in the workplace or within the family. Your life may sometimes be taken along the path of either happiness or unhappiness when a new person comes into your life. You need to think about how to solve the problems caused by personal relations.

The closer you are to a person, the more effort you should make to establish a wonderful relationship. Rather than simply judging others from your own visceral likes and dislikes, you should always think about ways to establish better relationships with others.

Take, for example, a relationship between a wife and her mother-in-law. If each tried to find and praise the good points of the other, there would be no problems. Once a wife discovers her mother-in-law's good points, she should admire them without hesitation, and the mother-in-law should do the same for her son's wife. If they do this, they will be able to build a relationship of love and respect for each other.

However, if they each worry that the other might hurt them, the opposite situation will unfold. For example, the mother-in-law might complain that her son has changed for the worse since he got married and that his wife is not right for him. The wife will then be very sensitive to these negative feelings and come to dislike her mother-in-law; she will want to stay away from her. If, on the other hand, the wife hears her mother-in-law say that her son has a good wife, she will feel happy and like her.

This example again demonstrates that the minds of people are like mirrors that reflect each other's minds. So, to free yourself from the restraints of human relationships, you must accept the fact that the image you hold of others in the "mirror of your mind" is actually an image of you reflected back to yourself.

So, to solve relationship problems, you should first resolve to give to others, admire and praise them, and nurture their strong points. If you do this, you may sometimes receive goodwill in return. Simply put, overwhelming goodwill is necessary to eliminate the problems that arise in human relationships. I will talk about this further in the next section.

# 4

## Overwhelming Goodwill

In an office, for example, a subordinate may betray his boss regardless of how well the boss took care of him and praised him all the time. This is just like how the saying goes, "Bite the hand that feeds you." The boss may become angry and think, "I did so much for him, but he talked about me in a negative way. It's unforgivable," or "After all the encouragement I gave him, he talks to me in this way?" This is quite common. Some people are ungrateful. Many people become angry about the fact that they have done everything they could for someone but received nothing in return.

The same is true in parent-child relationships. Although parents believe they have done everything possible for their children, the children may not make any effort to show their gratitude once they have left home. This often results in parents feeling abandoned.

It is commonly seen in the world of arts and crafts, too. An apprentice will leave the nest of his master after training for several years to eventually become his rival. This is a common story. In a company, the president may spend years grooming someone to be his successor with great care, only to watch them leave the company to start a new business of their own as his competitor.

When this kind of thing happens, it is only natural to feel betrayed and taken advantage of. These sorts of emotions arise because the idea of "give-and-take" has infiltrated your mind. People unconsciously expect that if they give, they will be given in return and that someone they praise will come to like them.

To avoid this kind of disappointment, you need to have an attitude of solely giving. When you do someone a favor, you should not expect anything in return. Just give and forget the fact that you have given.

Unhappiness in life begins when you constantly remember what you have given to others and forget what others have given you. "Although I did so much for him, he didn't do anything for me in return"—your unhappiness starts when you think this way. People often think, "I did so much for him; I loved him and took good care of him, but he has done nothing for me in return. He does not appreciate me." However, these people need to be aware that in thoughts such as "I did it for him," there is a sense of immaturity. When you give to others, you should give for free. It is particularly true for kindness and consideration; you need to remind yourself that love for others is solely for giving and that it is a one-way transaction. If you happen to receive love in return, you should consider it an unexpected bonus.

Do not expect anything in return. Just give sincerely, and instantly forget about the fact that you gave. On the other hand, try to remember what others have done for you and feel grateful to them. There are so many ungrateful people in the world, and you should be aware that you are no exception. Although you may believe that you carved out your own path by yourself, it is an undeniable fact that you were given help from many people in the process. You have simply forgotten the goodwill and heartfelt love that you have received from your parents, teachers, friends, superiors, and colleagues. This is what makes you say things like, "No one has done anything for me" or "After all I did for him, he turned around and betrayed me. It's like I was bit by my own dog."

It is a fact that those who always remember what they did for others tend to be quick to forget what others did for them. When you do something for others, it is important to do so without expecting any kind of reward and to forget what you have done. At the same time, remember what others have done for you as long as you can and continue to feel grateful. If everyone adopted this basic way of thinking, the world would be a better place.

The problem with the idea of give-and-take is that it lacks the sense of overwhelming goodwill. You may have thoughts such as, "He said negative things about me even though I praised him" or "I helped him get ahead at work, but now he ignores me. This is outrageous." However, the fact that you feel this way means you do not have enough goodwill. You are assuming that if you are good to someone, it is only natural that the other person will treat you well, too. This shows that your sense of happiness is so small that it can be disturbed by what others think of you. In other words, you only feel satisfied when the goodwill or happiness that you give to others is returned to you. If you are filled with goodwill and happiness, you should be able to wash away all these negative thoughts.

Why can't you give unlimited goodwill and happiness? Why can't unlimited energy flow out from you like an overflowing spring? Look at Mother Nature. In the mountains, you can see numerous springs where the water comes gushing out abundantly. Do these springs ever ask for money? There are oases in the desert. Do they ask human beings for even one penny? They just provide water endlessly, quenching the thirst of travelers. When you buy pork or beef, you have to pay for it, but what do the cows or pigs ever get back in return? What are they given for sacrificing their lives? Have you ever thought about this?

What about the sun in the sky? Does it ever ask for something in return from human beings? Does it ask for even one penny? Electric power companies charge money for electricity, but the sun gives us heat and energy for free. It is probably impossible to expect mere human beings to be like the sun, but at least you need to be aware that, in Mother Nature, there are many overflowing blessings as such. In these blessings is Buddha's mercy.

You should learn to care less about the ungratefulness of others. If you care much about their ungratefulness, you need to be aware that you also have the idea of give-and-take and a petty, cowardly heart that depends on others' opinions of you to be happy. It is important to have a generous heart and to enrich people with overwhelming goodwill that gushes out like a spring.

If you feel hurt by the remarks of others and start complaining that you have not been rewarded or that other people are ungrateful to you, remember the words "overwhelming goodwill." You should ask yourself whether you have a heart that simply gives. If you are feeling frustrated at not receiving anything in return, you should not give anything in the first place. It would be better for you not to encourage others, not to have any intention of making them happy, but rather to be content just living inside your own shell.

Once you have decided to make other people happy and to help them improve themselves, you have to be determined just to give. Please remember that you should not expect anything in return. This is an important mindset.

# 5

## An Unshakable Mind

I have discussed "an unshakable mind" from different angles. In the end, the main issue is the quality and quantity of accomplishments we can leave for others in this lifetime. By "accomplishments" I do not necessarily mean business achievements; the way you live or your life itself is also an accomplishment. Whether you are a child or an adult, a man or a woman, just living out your life is great work in itself. You need to have an unshakable mind exactly for this reason: to complete this great work.

A mind that does not sway no matter what happens— this does not mean being narrow-minded or stubborn. It is a determination to complete your life's work no matter what may happen. The purer this determination is, the more heavenly life you are living.

By "an unshakable mind," I do not mean for you to be like a self-made president who is sometimes overconfident. I am not asking you to contribute to humanity with such an obstinate attitude. An unshakable mind must be founded upon your love for Buddha. You must feel love for Buddha and believe that you are one with the Creator of the Great Universe. You need to be aware that you have the same nature as the laws and energy that govern the Great

Universe and that you are a part of the energy of this Great Universe. This is what you are, and currently, this energy has its own unique character and is undergoing spiritual training in this world.

You are a fragment of Buddha, and you are given your current particular name just for this lifetime. So, your self-realization must represent a part of Buddha's character. This self-realization must include your resolve to realize Buddha's ideals in this world, no matter what obstacles you meet. This is the mindset that separates those who wrote great works or were considered teachers of life from ordinary people.

An unshakable mind is the mind that comes from being a part of Buddha. It is the mind to live in this world and to bring light into it on behalf of Buddha. It is the pure intention of creating a better world. The stronger and bigger your unshakable mind is, the higher the level you will be able to reach.

An unshakable mind is, after all, an indispensable anchor and energy for carrying out Buddha's sacred work, a work that reflects Buddha's Will on earth. On stormy nights, it serves as an enormously heavy iron anchor, and on fine days, it serves as a mast. This is the unshakable mind.

I would like every one of you to realize the ideals that spring from the depths of your heart, straightforwardly and wholeheartedly, without being swayed by life's minor difficulties or small worries. That is why I have written this book. I hope you will carefully read it over and over again, savor it, and absorb it as nourishment for your mind.

# *Afterword*

I have already published books on the systematic structure of Buddha's Truth, such as *The Laws of the Sun*, *The Golden Laws*, and *The Nine Dimensions*. Even so, the flame of enthusiasm that burns within me to spread Buddha's Truth grows ever so strongly and brighter.

In this book, I have focused on the idea of an unshakable mind. I sincerely believe that the Buddha's Truth that gushes forth from this new approach will provide many people with practical answers to help them overcome their worries.

The last chapter, "An Unshakable Mind," contains powerful words with spiritual power. May these words send my readers a strong wind to their "mast of life" and the strength to propel themselves across the ocean of suffering. That is my earnest wish.

*Ryuho Okawa*
*Master & CEO of Happy Science Group*
*June, 1997*

*For a deeper understanding of*
An Unshakable Mind
*see other books below by Ryuho Okawa:*


*The Laws of the Sun* [New York: IRH Press, 2018]
*The Golden Laws* [Tokyo: HS Press, 2015]
*The Nine Dimensions* [New York: IRH Press, 2012]

# ABOUT THE AUTHOR

Founder and CEO of Happy Science Group.

Ryuho Okawa was born on July 7th 1956, in Tokushima, Japan. After graduating from the University of Tokyo with a law degree, he joined a Tokyo-based trading house. While working at its New York headquarters, he studied international finance at the Graduate Center of the City University of New York. In 1981, he attained Great Enlightenment and became aware that he is El Cantare with a mission to bring salvation to all humankind.

In 1986, he established Happy Science. It now has members in 169 countries across the world, with more than 700 branches and temples as well as 10,000 missionary houses around the world.

He has given over 3,500 lectures (of which more than 150 are in English) and published over 3,150 books (of which more than 600 are Spiritual Interview Series), and many of which are translated into 41 languages. Along with *The Laws of the Sun* and *The Laws of Hell*, many of the books have become best sellers or million sellers. To date, Happy Science has produced 27 movies under the supervision of Okawa. He has given the original story and concept and is also the Executive Producer. He has also composed music and written lyrics of over 450 pieces.

Moreover, he is the Founder of Happy Science University and Happy Science Academy (Junior and Senior High School), Founder and President of the Happiness Realization Party, Founder and Honorary Headmaster of Happy Science Institute of Government and Management, Founder of IRH Press Co., Ltd., and the Chairperson of NEW STAR PRODUCTION Co., Ltd. and ARI Production Co., Ltd.

# BOOKS BY RYUHO OKAWA

## Personal Growth Titles

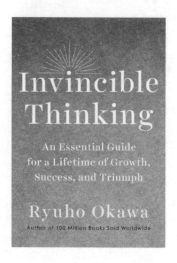

## Invincible Thinking

An Essential Guide for a Lifetime of Growth, Success, and Triumph

Hardcover • 208 pages • $16.95
ISBN: 978-1-942125-25-9 (Sep. 5, 2017)

When we encounter adversity, hardship or failure, how can we find the resilience and will to persevere? On the other hand, what can we do when everything is going well for us? It is our mental attitude that determines whether we can realize continuous growth and joyful achievement in any circumstance.

In this book, Ryuho Okawa lays out the principles of invincible thinking that will allow us to achieve long-lasting triumph. This powerful and unique philosophy is not only about becoming successful or achieving our goal in life, but also about building the foundation of life that becomes the basis of our life-long, lasting success and happiness.

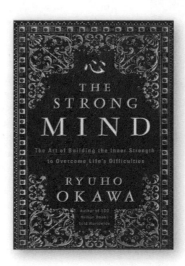

## The Strong Mind

The Art of Building the Inner Strength to Overcome Life's Difficulties

Paperback • 192 pages • $15.95
ISBN: 978-1-942125-36-5 (May 25, 2018)

The strong mind is what we need to rise time and again, and to move forward no matter what difficulties we face in life.

In this book, Ryuho Okawa presents a self-transformative perspective on life's hardships and challenges as precious opportunities for inner growth. It will inspire and empower you to take courage, develop a mature and cultivated heart, and achieve resilience and hardiness so that you can break through the barriers of your limits. With this book as your guide, life's challenges will become treasures that bring lasting and continuous enrichment to your soul.

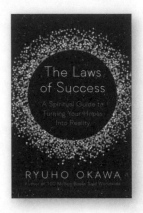

## The Laws of Success

A Spiritual Guide to Turning
Your Hopes Into Reality

Paperback • 208 pages • $15.95
ISBN: 978-1-942125-15-0 (Mar. 15, 2017)

*The Laws of Success* offers 8 spiritual principles that, when put to practice in our day-to-day life, will help us attain lasting success. The timeless wisdom and practical steps that Ryuho Okawa offers will guide us through any difficulties and problems we may face in life, and serve as guiding principles for living a positive, constructive, and meaningful life.

## The Laws of Happiness

Love, Wisdom, Self-Reflection and
Progress

Paperback • 264 pages • $16.95
ISBN: 978-1-942125-70-9 (Aug. 28, 2020)

Happiness is not found outside us; it is found within us. It is in how we think, how we look at our lives, and how we devote our hearts to the work we do. Discover how the Fourfold Path of Love, Wisdom, Self-Reflection and Progress creates a life of sustainable happiness.

## Worry-Free Living

Let Go of Stress and
Live in Peace and Happiness

Hardcover • 192 pages • $16.95
ISBN: 978-1-942125-51-8 (May 15, 2019)

The wisdom Ryuho Okawa shares in this book about facing problems in human relationships, financial hardships, and other life's stresses will help you change how you look at and approach life's worries and problems for the better. Let this book be your guide to finding precious meaning in all your life's problems, gaining inner growth and practicing inner happiness and spiritual growth.

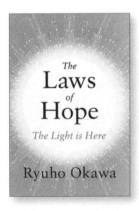

## The Laws of Hope

The Light is Here

Paperback • 224 pages • $16.95
ISBN:978-1-942125-76-1 (Jan. 15, 2021)

This book provides ways to bring light and hope to ourselves through our own efforts, even in the midst of sufferings and adversities. Inspired by a wish to bring happiness, success, and hope to humanity, Ryuho Okawa shows us how to look at and think about our lives and circumstances. By making efforts in your current circumstances, you can fulfill your mission to shed light on yourself and those around you.

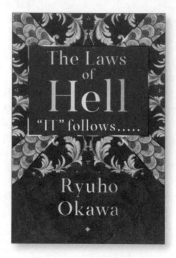

## The Laws of Hell

"IT" follows.....

Paperback • 264 pages • $17.95
ISBN: 978-1-958655-04-7 (May 1, 2023)

Whether you believe it or not, the Spirit World and hell do exist. Currently, the Earth's population has exceeded 8 billion, and unfortunately, 1 in 2 people are falling to hell.

This book is a must-read at a time like this since more and more people are unknowingly heading to hell; the truth is, new areas of hell are being created, such as 'internet hell' and 'hell on earth.' Also, due to the widespread materialism, there is a sharp rise in the earthbound spirits wandering around Earth because they have no clue about the Spirit World.

To stop hell from spreading and to save the souls of all human beings, Ryuho Okawa has compiled vital teachings in this book. This publication marks his 3,100th book and is the one and only comprehensive Truth about the modern hell.

### The Truth about Spiritual Phenomena
Life's Q&A With El Cantare

Paperback • 232 pages • $17.95
ISBN: 978-1-958655-0-92 (Oct. 27, 2023)

These are the records of Ryuho Okawa's answers to 26 questions related to spiritual phenomena and mental health, which were conducted live during his early public lectures with the audience. With his great spiritual ability, he revealed the unknown spiritual Truth behind the spiritual phenomena.

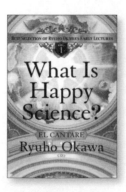

### What Is Happy Science?
Best Selection of Ryuho Okawa's Early Lectures (Volume 1)

Paperback • 256 pages • $17.95
ISBN: 978-1-942125-99-0 (Aug. 25, 2023)

The Best Selection series is a collection of Ryuho Okawa's passionate lectures during the ages of 32 to 33 that reveal the mission and goal of Happy Science. This book contains the eternal Truth, including the meaning of life, the secret of the mind, the true meaning of love, the mystery of the universe, and how to end hatred and world conflicts.

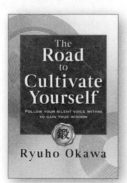

### The Road to Cultivate Yourself
Follow Your Silent Voice Within to Gain True Wisdom

Paperback • 256 pages • $17.95
ISBN: 978-1-958655-05-4 (Jun. 22, 2023)

In the age of uncertainty, how should we live our lives?

This book offers unchanging Truth in the ever-changing world, such as the secrets to become more aware about the spiritual self and how to increase intellectual productivity amidst the rapid changes of the modern age. It is packed with Ryuho Okawa's crystallized wisdom of life.

## The Essence of Buddha

The Path to Enlightenment

Paperback • 208 pages • $14.95
ISBN: 978-1-942125-06-8 (Oct. 1, 2016)

In this book, Ryuho Okawa imparts in simple and accessible language his wisdom about the essence of Shakyamuni Buddha's philosophy of life and enlightenment–teachings that have been inspiring people all over the world for over 2,500 years. By offering a new perspective on core Buddhist thoughts that have long been cloaked in mystique, Okawa brings these teachings to life for modern people. *The Essence of Buddha* distills a way of life that anyone can practice to achieve a life of self-growth, compassionate living, and true happiness.

## The True Eightfold Path

Guideposts for Self-Innovation

Paperback • 256 pages • $16.95
ISBN: 978-1-942125-80-8 (Mar. 30, 2021)

This book explains how we can apply the Eightfold Path, one of the main pillars of Shakyamuni Buddha's teachings, as everyday guideposts in the modern-age to achieve self-innovation to live better and make positive changes in these uncertain times.

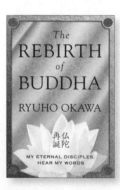

## The Rebirth of Buddha

My Eternal Disciples, Hear My Words

Paperback • 280 pages • $17.95
ISBN: 978-1-942125-95-2 (Jul. 15, 2022)

These are the messages of Buddha who has returned to this modern age as promised to his eternal beloved disciples. They are in simple words and poetic style, yet contain profound messages. Once you start reading these passages, you will remember why you chose to be born in the same era as Buddha. Listen to the voices of your Eternal Master and awaken to your calling.

## The Challenge of Enlightenment

Now, Here, the New Dharma Wheel Turns

Paperback • 380 pages • $17.95
ISBN: 978-1-942125-92-1 (Dec. 20, 2022)

Buddha's teachings, a reflection of his eternal wisdom, are like a bamboo pole used to change the course of your boat in the rapid stream of the great river called life. By reading this book, your mind becomes clearer, learns to savor inner peace, and it will empower you to make profound life improvements.

The Laws Series is an annual volume of books that are comprised of Ryuho Okawa's core teachings that function as universal guidance to all people. They are of various topics that were given in accordance with the changes that each year brings. *The Laws of the Sun*, the first publication of the laws series, ranked in the annual best-selling list in Japan in 1994. Since, the laws series' titles have ranked in the annual best-selling list every year for more than two decades, setting socio-cultural trends in Japan and around the world.

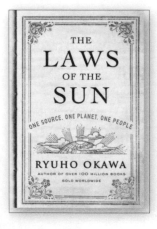

## The Laws of the Sun

One Source, One Planet, One People

Paperback • 288 pages • $15.95
ISBN: 978-1-942125-43-3 (Oct. 25, 2018)

IMAGINE IF YOU COULD ASK GOD why He created this world and what spiritual laws He used to shape us—and everything around us. The truth behind the creation of the universe is revealed in this book. If we could understand His designs and intentions, we could discover what our goals in life should be and whether our actions move us closer to those goals or farther away.

At a young age, a spiritual calling prompted Ryuho Okawa to outline what he innately understood to be universal truths for all humankind. In *The Laws of the Sun*, Okawa outlines these laws of the universe and provides a road map for living one's life with greater purpose and meaning. In this powerful book, Ryuho Okawa reveals the transcendent nature of consciousness and the secrets of our multidimensional universe and our place in it. By understanding the different stages of love and following the Buddhist Eightfold Path, he believes we can speed up our eternal process of development. *The Laws of the Sun* shows the way to realize true happiness—a happiness that continues from this world through the other.

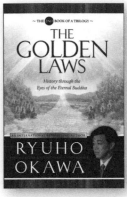

## The Golden Laws

History through the Eyes of
the Eternal Buddha

E-book • 204 pages • $13.99
ISBN: 978-1-941779-82-8 (Sep. 24, 2015)

Throughout history, Great Guiding Spirits of Light have been present on Earth in both the East and the West at crucial points in human history to further our spiritual development. *The Golden Laws* reveals how Divine Plan has been unfolding on Earth, and outlines 5,000 years of the secret history of humankind. Once we understand the true course of history, through past, present and into the future, we cannot help but become aware of the significance of our spiritual mission in the present age.

## The Nine Dimensions

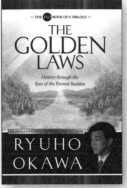

Unveiling the Laws of Eternity

Paperback • 168 pages • $15.95
ISBN: 978-0-982698-56-3 (Feb. 16, 2012)

This book is a window into the mind of our loving God, who designed this world and the vast, wondrous world of our afterlife as a school with many levels through which our souls learn and grow. When the religions and cultures of the world discover the truth of their common spiritual origin, they will be inspired to accept their differences, come together under faith in God, and build an era of harmony and peaceful progress on Earth.

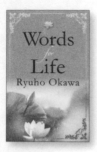

### Words for Life

Paperback • 136 pages • $15.95
ISBN: 979-8-88727-089-7 (Mar. 16, 2023)

Ryuho Okawa has written over 3,150 books on various topics. To help readers find the teachings that are beneficial for them out of the extensive teachings, the author has written 100 phrases and put them together. Inside you will find words of wisdom that will help you improve your mindset and lead you to live a meaningful and happy life.

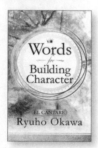

### Words for Building Character

Paperback • 140 pages • $15.95
ISBN: 979-8-88737-091-0 (Jun. 21, 2023)

When your life comes to an end, what you can bring with you to the other world is your enlightenment, in other words, the character that you build in this lifetime. If you can read, relish, and truly understand the meaning of these religious phrases, you will be able to attain happiness that transcends this world and the next.

### Words to Read in Times of Illness

Hardcover • 136 pages • $17.95
ISBN: 978-1-958655-07-8 (Sep. 15, 2023)

Ryuho Okawa has written 100 Healing Messages to comfort the souls of those going through any illness. When we are ill, it is an ideal time for us to contemplate recent and past events, as well as our relationship with people around us. It is a chance for us to take inventory of our emotions and thoughts.

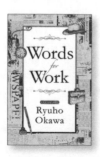

### Words for Work

Paperback • 140 pages • $15.95
ISBN: 979-8-88737-090-3 (Jul. 20, 2023)

Through his personal experiences at work, Okawa has created these phrases regarding philosophies and practical wisdom about work. This book will be of great use to you throughout your career. Every day you can contemplate and gain tips on how to better your work as well as to deepen your insight into company management.

## Other Recommended Titles

### THE UNHAPPINESS SYNDROME
28 Habits of Unhappy People (and How to Change Them)

### THE STARTING POINT OF HAPPINESS
An Inspiring Guide to Positive Living with Faith,
Love, and Courage

### THE MIRACLE OF MEDITATION
Opening Your Life to Peace, Joy, and the Power Within

### THE ROYAL ROAD OF LIFE
Beginning Your Path of Inner Peace, Virtue, and
a Life of Purpose

### TWICEBORN
My Early Thoughts that Revealed My True Mission

### THE LAWS OF SECRET
Awaken to This New World and Change Your Life

### SPIRITUAL WORLD 101
A Guide to a Spiritually Happy Life

### THE CHALLENGE OF THE MIND
An Essential Guide to Buddha's Teachings:
Zen, Karma, and Enlightenment

### THE POWER OF BASICS
Introduction to Modern Zen Life
of Calm, Spirituality and Success

*For a complete list of books, visit okawabooks.com*

# WHO IS EL CANTARE?

El Cantare means "the Light of the Earth." He is the Supreme God of the Earth who has been guiding humankind since the beginning of Genesis, and He is the Creator of the universe. He is whom Jesus called Father and Muhammad called Allah, and is *Ame-no-Mioya-Gami*, Japanese Father God. Different parts of El Cantare's core consciousness have descended to Earth in the past, once as Alpha and another as Elohim. His branch spirits, such as Shakyamuni Buddha and Hermes, have descended to Earth many times and helped to flourish many civilizations. To unite various religions and to integrate various fields of study in order to build a new civilization on Earth, a part of the core consciousness has descended to Earth as Master Ryuho Okawa.

**Alpha** is a part of the core consciousness of El Cantare who descended to Earth around 330 million years ago. Alpha preached Earth's Truths to harmonize and unify Earth-born humans and space people who came from other planets.

**Elohim** is a part of the core consciousness of El Cantare who descended to Earth around 150 million years ago. He gave wisdom, mainly on the differences of light and darkness, good and evil.

**Ame-no-Mioya-Gami (Japanese Father God)** is the Creator God and the Father God who appears in the ancient literature, *Hotsuma Tsutae*. It is believed that He descended on the foothills of Mt. Fuji about 30,000 years ago and built the Fuji dynasty, which is the root of the Japanese civilization. With justice as the central pillar, Ame-no-Mioya-Gami's teachings spread to ancient civilizations of other countries in the world.

**Shakyamuni Buddha** was born as a prince into the Shakya Clan in India around 2,600 years ago. When he was 29 years old, he renounced the world and sought enlightenment. He later attained Great Enlightenment and founded Buddhism.

**Hermes** is one of the 12 Olympian gods in Greek mythology, but the spiritual Truth is that he taught the teachings of love and progress around 4,300 years ago that became the origin of the current Western civilization. He is a hero that truly existed.

**Ophealis** was born in Greece around 6,500 years ago and was the leader who took an expedition to as far as Egypt. He is the God of miracles, prosperity, and arts, and is known as Osiris in the Egyptian mythology.

**Rient Arl Croud** was born as a king of the ancient Incan Empire around 7,000 years ago and taught about the mysteries of the mind. In the heavenly world, he is responsible for the interactions that take place between various planets.

**Thoth** was an almighty leader who built the golden age of the Atlantic civilization around 12,000 years ago. In the Egyptian mythology, he is known as God Thoth.

**Ra Mu** was a leader who built the golden age of the civilization of Mu around 17,000 years ago. As a religious leader and a politician, he ruled by uniting religion and politics.

# ABOUT HAPPY SCIENCE

Happy Science is a religious group founded on the faith in El Cantare who is the God of the Earth, and the Creator of the universe. The essence of human beings is the soul that was created by God, and we all are children of God. God is our true parent, so in our souls we have a fundamental desire to "believe in God, love God, and get closer to God." And, we can get closer to God by living with God's Will as our own. In Happy Science, we call this the "Exploration of Right Mind." More specifically, it means to practice the Fourfold Path, which consists of "Love, Wisdom, Self-Reflection, and Progress."

**Love**: Love means "love that gives," or mercy. God hopes for the happiness of all people. Therefore, living with God's Will as our own means to start by practicing "love that gives."

**Wisdom**: By studying and putting spiritual knowledge into practice, you can cultivate wisdom and become better at resolving problems in life.

**Self-Reflection**: Once you learn the heart of God and the difference between His mind and yours, you should strive to bring your own mind closer to the mind of God—that process is called self-reflection. Self-reflection also includes meditation and prayer.

**Progress**: Since God hopes for the happiness of all people, you should also make progress in your love, and make an effort to realize utopia in which everyone in your society, country, and eventually all humankind can become happy.

As we practice this Fourfold Path, our souls will advance toward God step by step. That is when we can attain real happiness— our souls' desire to get closer to God comes true.

In Happy Science, we conduct activities to make ourselves happy through belief in Lord El Cantare, and to spread this faith to the world and bring happiness to all. We welcome you to join our activities!

*We hold events and activities to help you practice the Fourfold Path at our branches, temples, missionary centers and missionary houses*

Love: We hold various volunteering activities. Our members conduct missionary work together as the greatest practice of love.

Wisdom: We offer our comprehensive books collection, many of which are available online and at Happy Science locations. In addition, we give out numerous opportunities such as seminars or book clubs to learn the Truth.

Self-Reflection: We offer opportunities to polish your mind through self-reflection, meditation, and prayer. There are many cases in which members have experienced improvement in their human relationships by changing their own minds.

Progress: We also offer seminars to enhance your power of influence. Because it is also important to do well at work to make society better, we hold seminars to improve your work and management skills.

# "The True Words Spoken By Buddha"

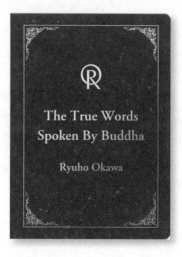

*The True Words Spoken By Buddha* is an English sutra given directly from the spirit of Shakyamuni Buddha, who is a part of Master Ryuho Okawa's subconscious. The words in this sutra are not of a mere human being but are the words of God or Buddha sent directly from the ninth dimension, which is the highest realm of the Earth's Spirit World.

*The True Words Spoken By Buddha* is an essential sutra for us to connect and live with God or Buddha's Will as our own.

# MEMBERSHIPS

## MEMBERSHIP

If you would like to know more about Happy Science, please consider becoming a member. Those who pledge to believe in Lord El Cantare and wish to learn more can join us.

When you become a member, you will receive the following sutra books: *The True Words Spoken By Buddha*, *Prayer to the Lord* and *Prayer to Guardian and Guiding Spirits*.

## DEVOTEE MEMBER

If you would like to learn the teachings of Happy Science and walk the path of faith, become a Devotee member who pledges devotion to the Three Treasures, which are Buddha, Dharma, and Sangha. Buddha refers to Lord El Cantare, Master Ryuho Okawa. Dharma refers to Master Ryuho Okawa's teachings. Sangha refers to Happy Science. Devoting to the Three Treasures will let your Buddha nature shine, and you will enter the path to attain true freedom of the mind.

Becoming a devotee means you become Buddha's disciple. You will discipline your mind and act to bring happiness to society.

---

✉ **EMAIL** OR ☎ **PHONE CALL**
Please see the contact information page.

📶 **ONLINE**  [ member.happy-science.org/signup/ 🔍 ]

# CONTACT INFORMATION

Happy Science is a worldwide organization with branches and temples around the globe. For a comprehensive list, visit the worldwide directory at happy-science.org. The following are some of our main Happy Science locations:

## UNITED STATES AND CANADA

### New York
79 Franklin St., New York, NY 10013, USA
Phone: 1-212-343-7972
Fax: 1-212-343-7973
Email: ny@happy-science.org
Website: happyscience-usa.org

### New Jersey
66 Hudson St., #2R, Hoboken, NJ 07030, USA
Phone: 1-201-313-0127
Email: nj@happy-science.org
Website: happyscience-usa.org

### Chicago
2300 Barrington Rd., Suite #400,
Hoffman Estates, IL 60169, USA
Phone: 1-630-937-3077
Email: chicago@happy-science.org
Website: happyscience-usa.org

### Florida
5208 8th St., Zephyrhills, FL 33542, USA
Phone: 1-813-715-0000
Fax: 1-813-715-0010
Email: florida@happy-science.org
Website: happyscience-usa.org

### Atlanta
1874 Piedmont Ave., NE Suite 360-C
Atlanta, GA 30324, USA
Phone: 1-404-892-7770
Email: atlanta@happy-science.org
Website: happyscience-usa.org

### San Francisco
525 Clinton St.
Redwood City, CA 94062, USA
Phone & Fax: 1-650-363-2777
Email: sf@happy-science.org
Website: happyscience-usa.org

### Los Angeles
1590 E. Del Mar Blvd., Pasadena,
CA 91106, USA
Phone: 1-626-395-7775
Fax: 1-626-395-7776
Email: la@happy-science.org
Website: happyscience-usa.org

### Orange County
16541 Gothard St. Suite 104
Huntington Beach, CA 92647
Phone: 1-714-659-1501
Email: oc@happy-science.org
Website: happyscience-usa.org

### San Diego
7841 Balboa Ave. Suite #202
San Diego, CA 92111, USA
Phone: 1-626-395-7775
Fax: 1-626-395-7776
E-mail: sandiego@happy-science.org
Website: happyscience-usa.org

### Hawaii
Phone: 1-808-591-9772
Fax: 1-808-591-9776
Email: hi@happy-science.org
Website: happyscience-usa.org

### Kauai
3343 Kanakolu Street, Suite 5
Lihue, HI 96766, USA
Phone: 1-808-822-7007
Fax: 1-808-822-6007
Email: kauai-hi@happy-science.org
Website: happyscience-usa.org

## Toronto
845 The Queensway
Etobicoke, ON M8Z 1N6, Canada
Phone: 1-416-901-3747
Email: toronto@happy-science.org
Website: happy-science.ca

## Vancouver
#201-2607 East 49th Avenue,
Vancouver, BC, V5S 1J9, Canada
Phone: 1-604-437-7735
Fax: 1-604-437-7764
Email: vancouver@happy-science.org
Website: happy-science.ca

## INTERNATIONAL

## Tokyo
1-6-7 Togoshi, Shinagawa,
Tokyo, 142-0041, Japan
Phone: 81-3-6384-5770
Fax: 81-3-6384-5776
Email: tokyo@happy-science.org
Website: happy-science.org

## London
3 Margaret St.
London, W1W 8RE United Kingdom
Phone: 44-20-7323-9255
Fax: 44-20-7323-9344
Email: eu@happy-science.org
Website: www.happyscience-uk.org

## Sydney
516 Pacific Highway, Lane Cove North,
2066 NSW, Australia
Phone: 61-2-9411-2877
Fax: 61-2-9411-2822
Email: sydney@happy-science.org

## Sao Paulo
Rua. Domingos de Morais 1154,
Vila Mariana, Sao Paulo SP
CEP 04010-100, Brazil
Phone: 55-11-5088-3800
Email: sp@happy-science.org
Website: happyscience.com.br

## Jundiai
Rua Congo, 447, Jd. Bonfiglioli
Jundiai-CEP, 13207-340, Brazil
Phone: 55-11-4587-5952
Email: jundiai@happy-science.org

## Seoul
74, Sadang-ro 27-gil,
Dongjak-gu, Seoul, Korea
Phone: 82-2-3478-8777
Fax: 82-2-3478-9777
Email: korea@happy-science.org

## Taipei
No. 89, Lane 155, Dunhua N. Road,
Songshan District, Taipei City 105, Taiwan
Phone: 886-2-2719-9377
Fax: 886-2-2719-5570
Email: taiwan@happy-science.org

## Taichung
No. 146, Minzu Rd., Central Dist.,
Taichung City 400001, Taiwan
Phone: 886-4-22233777
Email: taichung@happy-science.org

## Kuala Lumpur
No 22A, Block 2, Jalil Link Jalan Jalil Jaya
2, Bukit Jalil 57000,
Kuala Lumpur, Malaysia
Phone: 60-3-8998-7877
Fax: 60-3-8998-7977
Email: malaysia@happy-science.org
Website: happyscience.org.my

## Kathmandu
Kathmandu Metropolitan City,
Ward No. 15, Ring Road, Kimdol,
Sitapaila Kathmandu, Nepal
Phone: 977-1-537-2931
Email: nepal@happy-science.org

## Kampala
Plot 877 Rubaga Road, Kampala
P.O. Box 34130 Kampala, UGANDA
Email: uganda@happy-science.org

# ABOUT IRH PRESS USA

IRH Press USA Inc. was founded in 2013 as an affiliated firm of IRH Press Co., Ltd., based in New York. The press exclusively publishes comprehensive titles by Ryuho Okawa, an international bestselling author who has written more than 3,150 titles on Self-Improvement, Spiritual Truth, Religious Truth and more, with 100 million copies sold worldwide. For more information, visit okawabooks.com.

*Follow us on:*

**f** Facebook: Okawa Books   **◎** Instagram: OkawaBooks
**▶** Youtube: Okawa Books   **✔** Twitter: Okawa Books
**𝓟** Pinterest: Okawa Books   **g** Goodreads: Ryuho Okawa

——— **NEWSLETTER** ———

To receive book related news, promotions and events, please subscribe to our newsletter below.

🔗 irhpress.com/pages/subscribe

——— **AUDIO / VISUAL MEDIA** ———

**YOUTUBE**    **PODCAST**

Introduction of Ryuho Okawa's titles; topics ranging from self-help, current affairs, spirituality, religion, and the universe.